Troubleshooting System Center Configuration Manager

Troubleshoot all the aspects of your Configuration Manager installation, from basic easy checks to the advanced log files and serious issues

Peter Egerton

Gerry Hampson

PACKT PUBLISHING enterprise

professional expertise distilled

BIRMINGHAM - MUMBAI

Troubleshooting System Center Configuration Manager

First published: March 2016

Production reference: 1230316

Published by Packt Publishing Ltd.
Livery Place
35 Livery Street
Birmingham B3 2PB, UK.

ISBN 978-1-78217-484-4

www.packtpub.com

Credits

Authors
Peter Egerton

Gerry Hampson

Reviewers
Nicolai Henriksen, Configmgr
MVP

Gert Lievens

Nicolas Milbrand

Randall Smith

Commissioning Editor
Veena Pagare

Acquisition Editors
Tushar Gupta

James Jones

Content Development Editor
Sanjeet Rao

Technical Editor
Shivani Kiran Mistry

Copy Editor
Sameen Siddiqui

Project Coordinator
Judie Jose

Proofreader
Safis Editing

Indexer
Monica Ajmera Mehta

Graphics
Disha Haria

Production Coordinator
Nilesh Mohite

Cover Work
Nilesh Mohite

About the Authors

Peter Egerton is a senior cloud consultant at Inframon Ltd in the UK. He has been working in IT since 2000, and through IT support roles has progressed into IT consultancy. He is also a Microsoft Certified Trainer. Peter has worked with some of the biggest organizations across Europe and the Middle East in a multitude of markets on their Configuration Manager and wider System Center designs, implementations, and support requirements. In his spare time, Peter is also a Community Leader at Windows Management User Group (WMUG) in the UK.

First and foremost, I would like thank my family for allowing me the time and giving me the support to complete this book. I'd like to thank my wife, Anna, and son, Adam, without whom none of this would be possible. Mum and Dad, Chris and Harry, thanks for all your help over the years, it means a lot. I'd like to thank my coauthor, Gerry Hampson, for helping me with this project; without him, this would not be possible. Thanks to my Inframon and WMUG colleagues for helping me progress and get better at what I do. Finally, I must thank the guys at Packt for all their hard work and patience throughout this project.

For me, this has been a challenging time personally whilst writing parts of this book; as a result, I will be donating all my proceeds to a UK charity for stillbirth, premature birth, and miscarriage. Thank you for buying this book.

Gerry Hampson is a senior consultant engineer with over twenty years of experience as an IT professional. He has worked for Ergo Group, which has been based in Dublin, Ireland, for almost 10 years. Gerry specializes in designing and deploying Microsoft technologies, with a particular interest in System Center Configuration Manager and Intune. He has been awarded Microsoft Most Valuable Professional (MVP) in Enterprise Client Management for 2015.

Gerry has a popular blog where he shares Enterprise Client Management tips with the community at large (`http://gerryhampsoncm.blogspot.in/`).

This is Gerry's first book. He hopes to author many more in the future.

I'd like to thank my lovely wife, Úna, for her everlasting support. Without her patience and understanding, I would not be able to engage in so much community activity.

I'd also like to thank Lauren Vivash for her inspiration.

About the Reviewers

Nicolai Henriksen, Configmgr MVP works as a chief consultant in Norway and has been for the last seventeen years now. He is among the few that have attained the MVP title in the most comprehensive and most used management system in the world, Configmgr.

Nicolai has been working on Configmgr projects for many customers over the past ten years now and has got quite a few skills in setting up and configuring the system, as well as troubleshooting when things go wrong.

Gert Lievens is currently active as a freelance consultant who has had the opportunity to design, implement, and maintain solutions for multiple large enterprises. He has almost 10 years of experience in Wintel environments, with the past years a strong focus on products in the Microsoft System Center suite and SQL Server.

In his spare time, Gert likes to keep busy with his photography, cooking, technology, and multimedia in general.

Nicolas Milbrand has over 12 years experience in IT. He started working with Configuration Manager (SCCM) since the 2003 release known as System Management Server 2003 (SMS 2003).

Nowadays, he works as a freelance consultant and trainer, specializing in System Center products, especially Operations Manager (SCOM) and Configuration Manager (SCCM).

He's also well acquainted with the other products of the System Center suite and other related technologies. He helps his customers to design, implement, and optimize their System Center infrastructures.

He was awarded Microsoft Most Valuable Professional (MVP) 5 times (2009 to 2013).

I want to thank my wife, Tiffany, who supported and encouraged me in spite of all the time it took me away from her to review this book.

Randall Smith is a senior systems administrator for Adams State University. He has been administering Windows, Linux, and BSD systems since 1999.

He has been active in helping other sysadmins solve problems online and off. He has presented at the Colorado Higher Ed Computing Organization and Educause conferences on topics including Linux KVM and the Ceph storage system.

www.PacktPub.com

eBooks, discount offers, and more

Did you know that Packt offers eBook versions of every book published, with PDF and ePub files available? You can upgrade to the eBook version at www.PacktPub. com and as a print book customer, you are entitled to a discount on the eBook copy. Get in touch with us at customercare@packtpub.com for more details.

At www.PacktPub.com, you can also read a collection of free technical articles, sign up for a range of free newsletters and receive exclusive discounts and offers on Packt books and eBooks.

https://www2.packtpub.com/books/subscription/packtlib

Do you need instant solutions to your IT questions? PacktLib is Packt's online digital book library. Here, you can search, access, and read Packt's entire library of books.

Why subscribe?

* Fully searchable across every book published by Packt
* Copy and paste, print, and bookmark content
* On demand and accessible via a web browser

Instant updates on new Packt books

Get notified! Find out when new books are published by following @PacktEnterprise on Twitter or the *Packt Enterprise* Facebook page.

Table of Contents

Preface

Microsoft System Center Configuration Manager is the most widely used product to manage enterprise and corporate client PCs worldwide. This book contains all the information that any Configuration Manager administrator requires to troubleshoot their installation of the product. This includes the infrastructure and hierarchy that forms the foundation of the structure of the product and its design, the roles that provide the many features of Configuration Manager, and not to forget, the clients themselves. We will also see which tools we can use to troubleshoot various components, how to recover from failures, and also how to avoid them in the first place.

Configuration Manager has grown to become a big product and not everyone will use all the components, so this book serves as a guide both for those of you who are new to the product and also those with experience. There are tips and references provided throughout this book, and there is something to learn for all of you.

What this book covers

Chapter 1, *The Configuration Manager Troubleshooting Toolkit*, discusses the most commonly used tools for troubleshooting a variety of problems that can be seen in Configuration Manager. This will give you a good insight into certain tools, which will be referred to later in the book when we take a look at specific roles.

Chapter 2, *Configuration Manager Monitoring Workspace and Log Files*, provides a high-level view of available log files, their locations, what they relate to, and what they typically contain. Specific examples of log files will be referred to in more detail in later chapters when dealing with specific Configuration Manager roles. Configuration Manager is well known for its hundreds of log files, so a reference list with real-world accompaniments is provided.

Chapter 3, Troubleshooting Configuration Manager Clients, gives you an idea of the most problematic areas with regards to clients which simply due to the client-server ratio is the largest component of a Configuration Manager installation. You will walk through some best practices for installation, along with how to work out where the client is failing and what to do about it. You will also take a look at some commonly seen issues and their resolutions.

Chapter 4, Troubleshooting Hierarchies and Site Servers, explains the most commonly implemented hierarchies and the problems that are often associated with them, where to look, and how to improve these hierarchies for best performance. This will include Configuration Manager servers, Active Directory and SQL Server, and the Configuration Manager console. Each topic will cover typical problems, how to solve them, where to look for them, and ways to improve performance.

Chapter 5, Troubleshooting Management Points and Distribution Points, explains how to troubleshoot the management point which is one of the key components of Configuration Manager. This chapter will give you details about how the management point works and where typical problems can occur. The distribution point is also a key component in Configuration Manager and can be a frequent cause of problems due to its function. The chapter will run through how a distribution point works, what to look out for, and how to resolve common issues.

Chapter 6, Troubleshooting Other Roles, explores the other roles in Configuration Manager including common issues, which log files to check, and how they can manifest or affect the rest of Configuration Manager. These roles work in different ways and you will learn how best to troubleshoot each one specifically.

Chapter 7, Troubleshooting Common Tasks, you will look at issues that can commonly occur during everyday use of Configuration Manager and what we can do to best resolve these. Using the methods and tools from previous chapters you will see how these can be applied to common problems.

Chapter 8, Disaster Recovery, we will explore what is actually in a backup, what the options are in the case of a Configuration Manager failure and how to recover from a disaster should the need arise.

Chapter 9, Avoiding Trouble, explains what can be done to actually avoid having to troubleshoot in the first place. This includes best practices for common tasks and how to maintain a healthy Configuration Manager installation.

Who this book is for

If you are new to Configuration Manager or have some experience with it, and are interested in identifying, diagnosing, and resolving the System Center Configuration Manager administration issues, then this book is for you.

Conventions

In this book, you will find a number of text styles that distinguish between different kinds of information. Here are some examples of these styles and an explanation of their meaning.

Code words in text, database table names, folder names, filenames, file extensions, pathnames, dummy URLs, user input, and Twitter handles are shown as follows: "In Configuration Manager 2012 versions, we are provided with `CMTrace.exe`."

A block of code is set as follows:

```
Wmic computersystem get manufacturer,model,name
```

Any command-line input or output is written as follows:

```
Manufacturer          Model                     Name
Microsoft Corporation  Surface with Windows 8 Pro    Surface-Pro
```

New terms and **important words** are shown in bold. Words that you see on the screen, for example, in menus or dialog boxes, appear in the text like this: "It can be started from the **Run** dialog or from a Command Prompt"

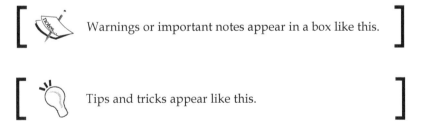

Warnings or important notes appear in a box like this.

Tips and tricks appear like this.

Reader feedback

Feedback from our readers is always welcome. Let us know what you think about this book—what you liked or disliked. Reader feedback is important for us as it helps us develop titles that you will really get the most out of.

To send us general feedback, simply e-mail `feedback@packtpub.com`, and mention the book's title in the subject of your message.

If there is a topic that you have expertise in and you are interested in either writing or contributing to a book, see our author guide at `www.packtpub.com/authors`.

Customer support

Now that you are the proud owner of a Packt book, we have a number of things to help you to get the most from your purchase.

Downloading the color images of this book

We also provide you with a PDF file that has color images of the screenshots/diagrams used in this book. The color images will help you better understand the changes in the output. You can download this file from `http://www.packtpub.com/sites/default/files/downloads/TroubleshootingSystemCenterConfigurationManager_ColorImages.pdf`.

Errata

Although we have taken every care to ensure the accuracy of our content, mistakes do happen. If you find a mistake in one of our books—maybe a mistake in the text or the code—we would be grateful if you could report this to us. By doing so, you can save other readers from frustration and help us improve subsequent versions of this book. If you find any errata, please report them by visiting `http://www.packtpub.com/submit-errata`, selecting your book, clicking on the **Errata Submission Form** link, and entering the details of your errata. Once your errata are verified, your submission will be accepted and the errata will be uploaded to our website or added to any list of existing errata under the Errata section of that title.

To view the previously submitted errata, go to `https://www.packtpub.com/books/content/support` and enter the name of the book in the search field. The required information will appear under the **Errata** section.

Piracy

Piracy of copyrighted material on the Internet is an ongoing problem across all media. At Packt, we take the protection of our copyright and licenses very seriously. If you come across any illegal copies of our works in any form on the Internet, please provide us with the location address or website name immediately so that we can pursue a remedy.

Please contact us at copyright@packtpub.com with a link to the suspected pirated material.

We appreciate your help in protecting our authors and our ability to bring you valuable content.

Questions

If you have a problem with any aspect of this book, you can contact us at questions@packtpub.com, and we will do our best to address the problem.

1
The Configuration Manager Troubleshooting Toolkit

In order to successfully troubleshoot Configuration Manager, there are a number of tools that are recommended to always keep in your troubleshooting toolkit. These include a mixture of Microsoft tools, third-party tools, and some community developed tools. Best of all is that they are free. As could be expected with the broad scope of functionality within Configuration Manager, there are also quite a variety of different utilities out there, so we need to know where to use the right tool for the problem. We are going to take a look through some commonly used tools and some not so commonly used tools, then look at what they do and where we can use them. These are not necessarily the be-all and end-all but they will certainly help us get on the way to solving problems and undoubtedly save some time. In this chapter, we are going to cover the following topics:

- Microsoft System Center Configuration Manager Toolkit
- Microsoft System Center 2012 Configuration Manager Support Center
- WMI Tools
- Registry Editor
- Group Policy Tools
- CMTrace/Trace32/Notepad
- Error code lists
- PowerShell
- Telnet
- Wireshark
- Operations Manager Management Pack
- Community Tools

Microsoft System Center Configuration Manager Toolkit

OK, so this one might be a bit of a cheat as the 2012 R2 version is actually 15 tools rolled into 1. It is, however, a brilliant set of free tools from Microsoft for finding out what is going on under the hood both client side and server side. For those who have never seen this one before, following are the tools that we can find in the download (`https://www.microsoft.com/en-us/download/details.aspx?id=50012`):

Server tools

These tools are useful when troubleshooting Configuration Manager servers, specifically the following ones:

- **DP Job Queue Manager**: This one gives us a nice clear view of what jobs a distribution point has on its to-do list. It is very useful when there are content distribution issues.

- **Collection Evaluation Viewer**: Listed as CEViewer, this will show us behind the scenes of collection evaluations. If there are any problems with collection limiting and delays in evaluation, then this is the tool that will help.

- **Content Library Explorer**: This tool can be used to look at content distribution and validation of content on a distribution point. It allows us to perform distribution and validation of content in one simple console.

- **Security Configuration Wizard**: Intended for Server 2008 R2, this is designed to help us run the minimum required server roles and features in order to run Configuration Manager 2012 R2, therefore reducing the potential risk for malicious behavior. In a secure environment with compliancy requirements, this is ideal.

- **Content Library Transfer**: If we are in the position where we have distribution point content on a disk that has filled, then this tool will help move all distribution point content from one disk to another.

- **Content Ownership Tool**: This tool lets us move content between Configuration Manager sites. In a multiple site hierarchy, this can be ideal.

- **Role-Based Administration Modeling and Auditing Tool**: This is a useful tool for planning role-based access to Configuration Manager and, therefore, save troubleshooting time later down the line.

- **Run Metering Summarization Tool**: If we need to run a software metering summarization on an ad hoc basis and cannot wait for the next scheduled run, then this is the tool to use.

Client tools

These tools are useful when troubleshooting Configuration Manager clients, specifically the following ones:

- **Client Spy**: This utility allows us to check software distribution, inventory, and software metering on a client, locally or remotely, and we can also export to a file for further analysis.

- **Configuration Manager Trace Log Viewer**: More commonly known as CMTrace, we will cover this in more detail later in this chapter, but when we want to view log files, this is a great choice.

- **Deployment Monitoring Tool**: This is nice little tool for ad hoc troubleshooting on a client and it gives us a current status for client properties, deployments, and software updates, so we know exactly what client data Configuration Manager is working with.

- **Policy Spy**: This is a frequently used utility for analyzing the policy on a Configuration Manager client and making policy requests. This one can help us figure out why a client isn't doing what we expect it to be doing.

- **Power Viewer Tool**: This tool will help us troubleshoot the many different options available when it comes to power management on a Configuration Manager client. It is also useful for testing power policy changes.

- **Send Schedule Tool**: If we want to force ad hoc evaluation of a configuration baseline on a client, then this tool will help us do this. There are other ways but having this handy tool can save us lots of time.

- **Wakeup Spy**: If **Wake on LAN (WoL)** is enabled in an environment, then we will undoubtedly get to use this at some point. This tool lets us view information about client wakeup state and listens for wakeup requests.

Microsoft System Center 2012 Configuration Manager Support Center

We can download Microsoft System Center 2012 Configuration Manager Support Center at `https://www.microsoft.com/en-us/download/details.aspx?id=42645`.

This one is often a particular favorite for technical support or consultants who are asked to troubleshoot other Configuration Manager environments unknown to them. The free tool was released for public use by the Microsoft support team and is used by them to obtain a good overall picture of a Configuration Manager infrastructure from the client perspective. The Support Center Tool is made up of the following three tools:

- Configuration Manager Support Center
- Configuration Manager Support Center Viewer
- Log Viewer

The Configuration Manager Support Center can perform several functions. The first is data collection. Information about the client is bundled together and can then be sent off to someone else to investigate or simply allow us to collate lots of useful information for our own investigations. The information gathered is as follows:

- Log files
- Policy
- Certificates
- Client configuration collector
- Client registry
- Client WMI
- Troubleshooting
- Debug dumps
- Operating system

All this information is bundled together into a ZIP file that contains logs, debug dumps, and various XML files depending on the options we choose. This file can then be opened in the Configuration Manager Support Center Viewer, which we will come to shortly.

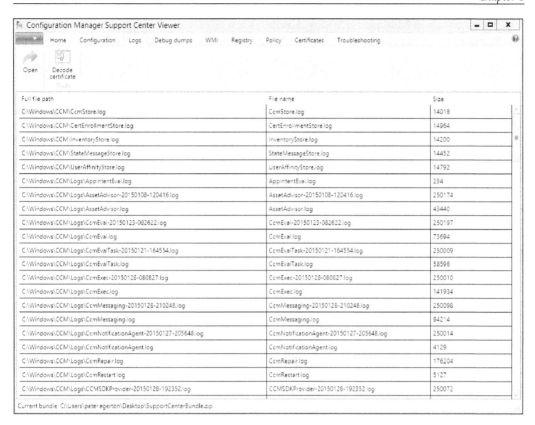

The Configuration Manager Support Center also allows us to load client information and control the agent service from one easy console. We can load, request, and evaluate policy, and listen for policy events in real time. Further functions enable us to work with, monitor, and manipulate client content cache for applications, software updates, and windows installers. There are also similar utilities for troubleshooting the various inventories available, software metering, and discovery data, and, finally, some log evaluation and common troubleshooting tasks. We will be revisiting some of these tools in more detail later in this book. In brief summary, this is a great one stop shop for client troubleshooting.

The Configuration Manager Support Center Viewer is the tool to use to open up the support bundle produced in the Configuration Manager Support Center. It splits all the gathered information into the respective categories and allows us or a completely remote person to browse the Configuration Manager logs, debug dumps, WMI repository, registry, policy, any gathered certificates, and the results of the troubleshooting tasks. Last but not least is the Log Viewer, which is used by default when we open any of the logs captured by the Configuration Manager Support Center, and it can be used as a generic log file viewer too. The feature set in the Log Viewer includes live updating, auto-scroll, a detail pane, wrapping of text, and a filter function on top of the standard facilities we would expect from any log viewer. All round, it is a really useful piece of software as it can make what can be often very detailed log files somewhat easier to read.

WMI tools

Windows Management Instrumentation (**WMI**) is rooted in Configuration Manager and the product has been using WMI since its early days when Configuration Manager was previously known as **System Management Server** (**SMS**). WMI was introduced in SMS 2.0 and has been used in the product for client and server functions in every version since. For this very reason, it is highly likely that we will need to take a look at WMI at some point on our troubleshooting journey. So with this in mind, it's important that we learn to use one of the various tools available to us. A simple example of WMI usage in Configuration Manager would be collection membership query rules that are made from **WMI Query Language** (**WQL**), which is a similar syntax to SQL. Effectively, what we are doing in these commands is querying a WMI database in much the same way as we might with a SQL database. For example, if we need to check a specific value in a client inventory, then we can do this with WMI. Another useful example is when working with configuration baselines as we can check specific values ad hoc and predict or confirm expected compliance or non-compliance. We shall mention just a few tools but this really is a personal preference, what it is used for and how you like to work.

Firstly, the **Windows Management Instrumentation Command Line** (**WMIC**) is a command line utility that can be run from a Command Prompt or PowerShell console that allows us to view and manipulate WMI from a command line, which means we can use it in scripts and automation products, and perform easy remote commands. It is a popular option with many as it offers additional scripting functionality which makes it particularly helpful outside of troubleshooting too. A basic example of the syntax used with WMIC would be the following query that will return the Manufacturer, Model, and Name of a machine from WMI:

```
Wmic computersystem get manufacturer,model,name
```

This would return something like the following when ran against, for example, a Microsoft Surface Pro:

```
Manufacturer            Model                      Name
Microsoft Corporation   Surface with Windows 8 Pro   Surface-Pro
```

This is a very basic common usage example of WMIC when trying to obtain the model number of a machine and is commonly used for a task sequence step condition to apply model specific drivers. We will reference WMIC later in this book and show where else this tool can be useful.

WBEMTest is another WMI tool but this time with a graphical user interface that again—like WMIC—allows us to dig deep into WMI and look at the classes, instances, and namespaces, as well as perform amendments. It can be started from the **Run** dialog or from a Command Prompt by simply typing:

```
Wbemtest
```

We are then presented with the **Windows Management Instrumentation Tester** window, as shown in the following screenshot, and we can make a connection into our preferred namespace:

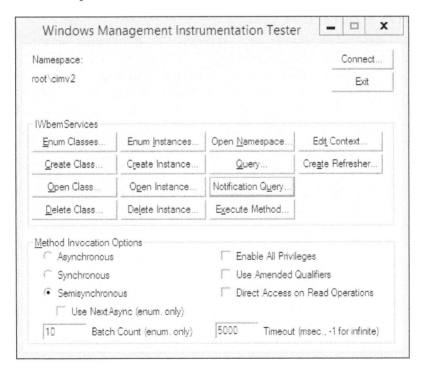

The main WMI namespace for a Configuration Manager client is root\CCM.

From here we can perform several tasks such as opening, enumerating, creating, and deleting classes and instances or performing queries. If we are performing ad hoc checks or simply prefer a point and click experience, then this could be the tool to use. However, along with the other WMI tools, we should know what we are looking for before getting too click happy, otherwise there is the potential to cause more damage than harm and give us more troubleshooting than we started with.

Finally, a brief introduction to the Microsoft mini-suite of WMI tools called **WMI Administrative Tools**: this is freely available in the download center and includes WMI CIM Studio, WMI Object Browser, WMI Event Registration Tool, and WMI Event Viewer. These tools mostly give away their function and, with the exception of the event viewer, offer us a browser-based view of WMI. These can be a good alternative to WMIC and WBEMTest as they can offer a wider view of WMI, which is often particularly useful for someone not overly familiar with the finer details of WMI.

Registry Editor

Also worth a mention is the Registry Editor that is built into Microsoft Windows on both server and client operating systems. Most IT administrators know this as regedit.exe and it is the default tool of choice for making any changes to or just simply viewing the contents of a registry key or value. Many of the Configuration Manager roles and the clients allow us to make changes to enable features such as extended logging or manually changing policy settings by using the registry to do so. It should be noted that changing the registry is not something that should be taken lightly as making incorrect changes can result in creating more problems not just in Configuration Manager but also in the operating system as a whole. If we stick to the published settings though we should be fine and this can be a fine tool when troubleshooting oddities and problems in a Configuration Manager environment.

Group Policy tools

A Configuration Manager is a client management tool; there are certain features and settings on a client such as software updates that may conflict with settings defined in Group Policy. Particularly in larger organizations, it can often be useful to compare and contrast the settings that may conflict between Group Policy and Configuration Manager. Using integrated tools, such a Resultant Set of Policy (RSoP) and Group Policy Result (`gpresult.exe`), or the Group Policy management console as part of the Remote Server Administration Tools (RSAT) can help identify where and why clients are not functioning as expected. We can then move forward and amend group policies as and where required using the Group Policy Object Editor. Used in combination, these tools can prove essential when dealing with Configuration Manager clients in particular.

Log file viewer

Those who have spent any time at all working with Configuration Manager will know that it contains quite a few log files, literally hundreds. We will go through the log files in more detail in the next chapter, but we will need to use something to read the logs. We can use something as simple as Notepad and to an extent there are some advantages with using this as it is a no-nonsense text reader. Having said that, generally speaking, most people want a little more when it comes to reading Configuration Manager logs as they can often be long, complex, and frequently refreshed. We have already seen one example of a log viewer as part of the Configuration Manager Support Center, but Configuration Manager includes its own log file viewer that is tailored to the needs of troubleshooting the product logs. In Configuration Manager 2012 versions, we are provided with `CMTrace.exe`; previous versions provided us with `Trace32.exe` or `SMSTrace.exe`. They are very similar tools but we will highlight some of the features of CMTrace, which is the more modern of the two. To begin with, we can typically find CMTrace at the following locations:

* `%ProgramFiles%\Microsoft Configuration manager\Tools\CMTrace.exe`
* `<INSTALLATION MEDIA>\SMSSETUP\TOOLS\CMTrace.exe`

Those who are running Configuration Manager 2012 R2 and up also have CMTrace available *out of the box* in WinPE when running Operating System Deployments. We can simply hit *F8* if we have command support enabled in the WinPE image and type CMTrace. This can also be added to the later stages of a task sequence when running in the full operating system by copying the file onto the hard disk. The single biggest advantage of using CMTrace over a standard text reader is that it is a tail reader that by default is refreshed every 500 milliseconds, or, in others words, it will update the window as new lines are logged in the log file; we also have the functionality to pause the file too. Other functionality of CMTrace is to allow filtering of the log based on certain conditions and there is also a highlight feature that can highlight a whole line in yellow if a word we are looking for is found on the line. The program automatically highlights lines if certain words are found such as error or warning, which is useful but can also be a red herring at times, so this is something to be aware of if we come across logs with these keywords. We can also merge log files, and this is particularly useful when looking at time critical incidents as we can analyze data from multiple sources in the order they happened and understand the flow of information between the different components.

Error code lists

When working with Microsoft technologies, we sometimes see the same error message used in different products. This makes a lot of sense because some products will use code from others and some will interact with others. Often overlooked is taking an error message from Configuration Manager and finding an unrelated example from another product. Let me give an example of HTTP. Many of the Configuration Manager roles are based on HTTP communication, and HTTP has a standard set of error messages. Add in some certificates and HTTPS communications and it is not unusual for people to start to get lost in the logs. What is often found is that if we take the error out of its Configuration Manager context for a moment and look at what that error means specifically in Internet Information Services (IIS), then this can help us understand what is happening, which can be applied back to our specific problem. This also works when searching on the Internet for error codes as it is something we all do as there is a breadth of information out there. We may well find that if we search for an error code on the Web, we can see the same error elsewhere; don't be put off and read it through as we might find it gives us that eureka moment.

With this in mind, we are not going to list every error code as this would be exhaustive; however, it is worthwhile bookmarking these standard lists that are recommended as being useful. Many of these error codes are also embedded into CMTrace and can be looked up through **Tools | Errors Lookup**.

- **Windows Installer Errors Reference**: This will help us understand the return codes from any Windows application or package deployments which is available at `http://msdn.microsoft.com/en-us/library/aa368371.aspx`.

- **HTTP Status Codes**: These are the standard status codes used by IIS and can prove particularly useful when troubleshooting the availability of IIS-based roles. More information is available at `http://support.microsoft.com/kb/943891`.

- **Custom Error Codes for Configuration Manager 2007**: Don't worry, this is not a typo; these are reference error codes for an old product version. This is because there is no formal published list for 2012 or current branch versions; however, you will find that the custom codes have changed very little, so this is still a great list to have. More information is available at `http://technet.microsoft.com/en-us/library/bb632794.aspx`.

PowerShell

PowerShell is here to stay. A phrase often heard recently is learn PowerShell or learn golf. Like it or not we cannot get away from the emphasis on this homemade product from Microsoft. This is evident in just about all current products as PowerShell is so deeply embedded. Configuration Manager is no exception to this, and although we cannot quite do everything we can in the console, there are an increasing number of cmdlets becoming available, more than 500 at the time of writing. So the question we may ask is "where does this come into troubleshooting?" Well for the uninitiated in PowerShell maybe it won't be the first tool they turn to but with some experience we can soon find that performing things like WMI queries and typical console tasks can be made quicker and slicker with PowerShell. If we prefer, we can also read log files from PowerShell and make remote changes to machines. PowerShell can be a one-stop shop for our troubleshooting needs if we spend time to pick up the skills.

Network tools

When we refer to networking tools, we are referring to everything ranging from a ping to a packet capture. When we break Configuration Manager down to its simplest form, we are trying to get data from point A to B, or server to client in other words. If we don't have a clear line of communication, then we are going to hit problems. Sounds simple right? We all know that it isn't always that easy in every organization. Often there are complex networks in place with routers and firewalls in between A and B, so it may not be clear what the problem can be. Add this to the combination of ports that Configuration Manager uses and it can be a recipe for confusion. The good thing about using network tools is that it is often a true or false scenario. A packet capture, for example, doesn't lie, it shows us exactly what is coming into and out of our network interface, which can be really powerful when looking into problems such as failed deployments, failed distribution, or Configuration Manager role installation. For these reasons, I think it is essential that we add some of the following utilities to our troubleshooting toolkit.

- **Ping**: This is almost too obvious and isn't guaranteed due to firewalling and devices dropping ICMP requests, but it is the first line in communication checks and often overlooked as a basic check and can also help check for any name resolution problems.

- **Tracert**: If we can run a trace route from point A to B, then this helps us rule this out or indeed rule in the point at which communications drop. Again, it is not a guaranteed result but certainly not worth forgetting about.

- **Telnet**: If we know there is a clear line of communication, then we can go a level further and try a Telnet to test the TCP ports out. Using our preferred Telnet client, we can simply run the following:

  ```
  telnet CMServer1 445
  ```

  This will test a connection from our source to our destination CMServer1 over TCP 445.

  If we want to use the default Microsoft Windows Telnet client, then don't forget we will need to enable this as a feature in modern operating systems.

- **Microsoft Message Analyzer**: Taking things a level deeper again, we can use this to capture packets at both sides of the communication chain and see what is or isn't being received and over what ports. This is the successor to Microsoft Network Monitor, and if we can master a tool like this, then it is often the last line port of call for communication issues as we can present the results to our network or firewall administrator and show them exactly what we need versus what we have. Another similar popular tool worth mentioning is Wireshark, previously known as Ethereal. There are several other tools out there to choose from, but this is a must have in our toolkit.

I have not specifically mentioned any of the other Command Prompt related tools that you can use but there are a handful of others that you may find useful. There is no steep learning curve involved with these, so if you are not already familiar, then take a little time out and see what they can do for you.

- `Pathping.exe`
- `Nbtstat.exe`
- `Netstat.exe`

For a full list of ports used by Configuration Manager, we should always refer to the TechNet library documentation as this is maintained by Microsoft and is definitive for a default installation of the product. The documentation is available at `https://technet.microsoft.com/en-gb/library/hh427328.aspx`.

System Center Configuration Manager Management Pack

You can find System Center Configuration Manager Management Pack at `https://www.microsoft.com/en-gb/download/details.aspx?id=29267`.

This one is not going to be applicable to everyone, but nonetheless I had to include it as a top troubleshooting tool. If you are not familiar with System Center Operations Manager, it is essentially the performance and monitoring tool in the System Center suite. Operations Manager is another Microsoft System Center product that will monitor servers, clients, network devices, and other things such as storage hardware and blade chassis with the use of management packs. This is not intended to be a lesson in Operations Manager, but essentially the management pack contains lots of detailed information about the ins and outs of a given application or service that will automatically discover and analyze the Configuration Manager infrastructure and highlight issues where necessary. This helps a lot not only with reactive scenarios as it can point out exactly where our problems lie, but also in proactive maintenance of our Configuration Manager environment as it can highlight potential failures before they happen and alert us accordingly. Management packs are often developed by the original software developer but there are often third-party versions available and with some experience we can even write our own. With regard to Configuration Manager then, what could be better than a management pack written by Microsoft that contains lots of low-level information about their own product? If this option is available, then it is highly recommended. Following is a summary of the monitoring we can find in the Configuration Manager Management pack:

- Replication health
- Configuration of replication
- Backup and recovery status monitor
- Component availability monitoring
- Service availability
- Server role availability monitoring
- Compliance rate of baseline deployment monitoring
- Discovery backlog monitoring
- General health monitoring
- Database connection monitoring
- Inventory backlog monitoring
- Software metering backlog monitoring
- Software update synchronization status monitoring
- Distribution point configuration monitoring

In addition, the following diagram shows us the monitored components and how they roll up to produce a health state in Operations Manager:

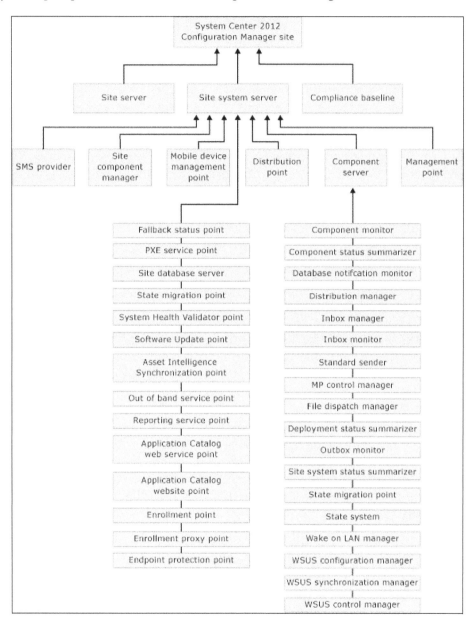

Having this management pack available to us can save so much time, both in the short and long term, when experiencing problems so again this has to go into the top picks for our troubleshooting toolkit.

Community contributions

Finally, as user group community leaders, we couldn't leave this section out of the troubleshooting toolkit. Configuration Manager has such a great collection of community contributors that have likely to have been through our troubleshooting pain before us and either blog about it, post it on a forum, or create a fix for it. There is such an array of free tools out there that people share that we cannot ignore them. Outside of troubleshooting specifically, some of the best add-ons available for Configuration Manager are community contributions, whether that be from individuals or businesses. There are so many utilities that are ever evolving and not all will suit your needs, but if we browse the Microsoft TechNet galleries, Codeplex, and GitHub, you are sure to find a great resource to meet your requirements. Why not get involved with a user group too? In terms of troubleshooting, this is probably one of the best things I personally could recommend. It gives access to a network of people who work on the same product as us and are often using them in the same way, so it is quite likely that someone has seen our problem before and can fast forward us to a solution.

- **Microsoft TechNet Galleries**: `https://gallery.technet.microsoft.com/`
- **Codeplex**: `https://www.codeplex.com/`
- **GitHub**: `https://github.com/`
- **Configuration Manager Community**: `http://go.microsoft.com/fwlink/p/?LinkId=626544`

Summary

In summary, our troubleshooting toolkit contains a variety of applications, all of which are free, and many of these tools will not take a great amount of time to get to grips with but will undoubtedly save us time so that is a great trade-off. Also included is something that isn't strictly a tool but can be just as important when trying to solve problems—product knowledge. It goes without saying that if we already understand how the product works, then our troubleshooting will generally be quicker and more successful. There aren't any training courses that will teach us how to deal with the unexpected that can sometimes occur in any software product, so fast-tracking that knowledge gain by getting involved with people in the know seems only logical. It can not only help us get over problems but also avoid them by improving our practices in the product to prevent problems in the future. In the next chapter, we will a look at the log files that underpin the troubleshooting of Configuration Manager and which files we would commonly use during everyday troubleshooting of this, sometimes overwhelming, product.

2
Configuration Manager Monitoring Workspace and Log Files

Key to troubleshooting any problem is information; if we do not have good information, how are we going to figure out what went wrong? We have all seen those comedy error messages that say something like *an error has occurred* and they just do not help the situation. Fortunately for us, Configuration Manager has really good status and error logging, which, for people who are new to the product, can often be off putting due to the level of detail. Even though the amount and level of detail of the log files can sometimes be overwhelming, it really is a matter of learning to read them and picking out that key piece of information that unlocks the mystery of the enigma. So with this in mind, this chapter sets out to help us in understanding the monitoring workspace in the Configuration Manager console and the log files, where they are, which one to use, and what they contain.

The Monitoring workspace

In Configuration Manager there are three levels of status checking on a sliding scale: from overview to part-detail and then finally detailed. The overview parts are the visual indicators in the console that consist of pie charts or high-level indicators that show distribution status, deployment status, and so on. The part-detailed are status message queries and the detailed are the log files. First of all, we are going to look at the monitoring workspace and see what we can use in there to help us with our troubleshooting.

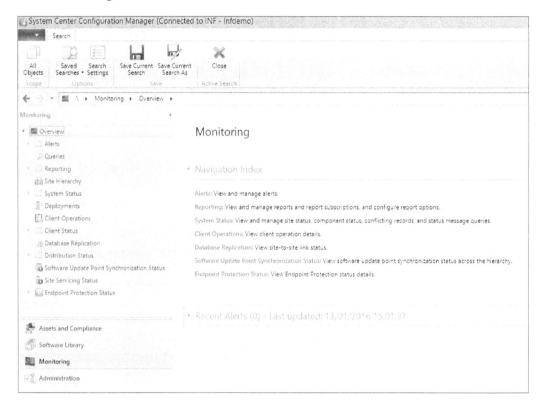

Alerts

While working from top to bottom in the monitoring workspace, the first thing we come across is **Alerts**. This can give us easy wins to common problems and, even better, we can set up e-mail subscriptions to notify us without being in the console.

In Configuration Manager 2012 without a service pack, we can only set e-mail subscriptions for Endpoint Protection alerts. In subsequent releases, SP1, R2 and current branch, we can add further e-mail subscriptions.

The alerts that are generated in this area of the console do not apply to every component of Configuration Manager, but still it is a quick hit to see if anything obvious has happened. If we look at the SQL database behind Configuration Manager, we can see in the `dbo.AlertClass` table from Configuration Manager current branch that the types of alert classes are limited and each one has a predefined severity. The messages that we will see in the console will be more descriptive and specific to our implementation, but this gives us an idea of the types of alerts we are likely to get.

Name	Severity
Apns expiration alert	1
Apple vpp token expiration alert	1
Apple vpp token near expiration alert	1
Cloud dp storage critical	1
Cloud dp traffic out critical	1
Database replication DLL loading error	1
Database replication link connectivity	1
Database replication message process rate critical	1
Database replication message transaction queue critical	1
Dcm compliance	1
Deployment compliance	1
Exchange connector	1
Malware detection	1
Malware outbreak	1
Migration job failure	1
Migration sync failure	1
Multiple malware detection	1
Osd-task sequences error exceeds threshold	1
Osd-task sequences success below threshold	1
Repeated malware detection	1
Rule failure	1
Site backup task failure	1

Name	Severity
Site role unhealthy	1
Site system database free space critical	1
Software updates sync failure	1
Sum-compliance1 update deployment success below threshold	1
Sum-compliance2 update group deployment success below threshold	1
Swd-app error exceeds threshold	1
Swd-app success below threshold	1
Cloud dp storage warning	2
Cloud dp traffic out warning	2
Collection membership	2
Database replication message process rate warning	2
Database replication message transaction queue warning	2
MDM_lowlicensekeys	2
Migration amt warning	2
Migration dp fqdn warning	2
Site system database free space warning	2
Symantec cert expiration alert	2
Client activity warning	3
Client health sla	3
Client remediation warning	3
Migration initial sync	3
Synthetic alert	3
Synthetic alert above double threshold	3
Synthetic alert above simple threshold	3
Synthetic alert below double threshold	3
Synthetic alert below simple threshold	3
Synthetic alert2	3

As we can see from the preceding alert names, there are a variety of components covered and each is evaluated by a whole host of SQL stored procedures that run behind the scenes. Do not be tempted to modify these stored procedures or tables at all; we are simply demonstrating that the views we see in the console are often reflective of a SQL table or view.

Before looking into the Configuration Manager database, you should have a working knowledge of Microsoft SQL. It is not supported to make any changes in the database as this can cause data corruption and potentially damage your Configuration Manager installation.

We can configure which alerts we would like to trigger in different places throughout the console; the key is to look for an alerts tab on the component properties. We can configure these in the site properties, on the management point properties, deployments, migrations, collection properties, and on anywhere else related to the aforementioned classes. If we want to configure alerts for clients in a specific device collection, we can go to the **Alerts** tab in the properties of the collection and click on **Add**, and we will see the various alerting options available to us, as shown in the following screenshot:

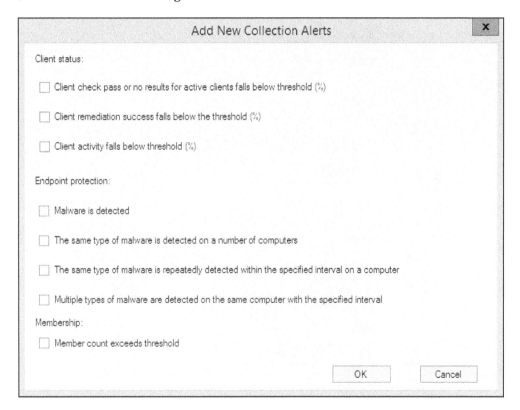

In terms of understanding these alerts, they are quite high level and in plain language, so they should give us an immediate steer as to where the problem lies. We can then take this steer and move forward to something like system status.

System status

In the system status section of the monitoring workspace, we have site status, component status, conflicting records, and status message queries. We will cover each area and how to use them in more detail when we look at the individual components. We are not going to cover the site hierarchy in any detail as it essentially gives us just a diagrammatical view of our site hierarchy. If, like the majority of implementations, you have a single site hierarchy, then this will be somewhat underwhelming as it will contain only a single server. If we right-click on the server, however, we will see a nice summary of the site status message with a hyperlink to drop us into the relevant view.

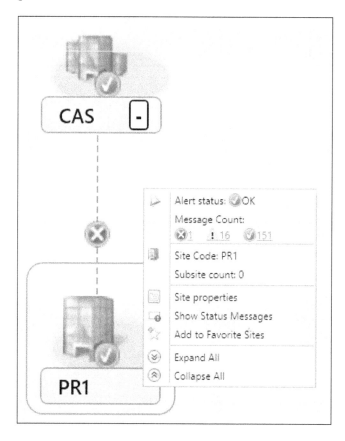

Moving further down the console under this section, we see the site status view that lists all the servers and server roles in our site along with a nice Error, Warning, or OK icon for each role. If you right-click on these or hit the ribbon you can view the relevant messages for that role and also start the Configuration Manager Service Manager. The Service Manager allows you to query the status of all components in the site and also components for a specific server, and, if required, we can easily restart individual components. Be careful while doing this, though, as we don't want to create unnecessary downtime when we are troubleshooting minor issues, and try to find out the root cause before getting click happy. There is an added treat in the Configuration Manager Service Manager in that you can browse through to the individual components, right-click, and hit logging. In here you can see the name of the log file for that specific component and amend the size of the log. This can be extremely helpful in some circumstances where log files are flushed before you had the chance to read that nugget of information. By default, log files are a maximum 2 MB, and when the file reaches that size, it is automatically stored with the .lo_ extension and the same file name, as shown in the following screenshot:

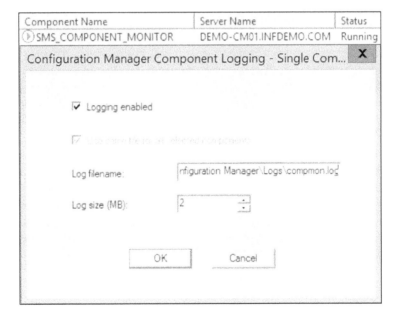

In the Component Status view, we see much of the same, but now we move into a more detailed view down to each individual component within our Configuration Manager site. In this view, the same applies again where we can drill down into the messages by type, and if we believe we have resolved the issue, we can reset the component to a healthy state by resetting the error count from here. It is worth noting at this point that we can amend the thresholds for each of the components by browsing to **Administration | Overview | Site Configuration | Sites**. Now we can right-click or go to the ribbon and hit **Status Summarizers**. In here we see listed the **Component Status Summarizer**, which we can edit, and amend thresholds for various components as appropriate for our environment. This can be very useful if you are experiencing re-occurring problems on a component as we can set the threshold low and pick up on the problem sooner. It should be noted that by default the thresholds reset at midnight, so any status seen in the console is since 00:00.

> When troubleshooting, it is important that we reset the counts for the relevant role or component each time we make a change. This will help us see what status messages are being produced without all the noise from old messages. If the problem persists, then the status message will appear again.

We may notice that when we drill down to message types, we are asked to choose a time period and we are presented with a separate window for the status message viewer. Alternatively, we can go straight into the status message queries view in the monitoring workspace. In here we can view what could be classed as the mid-level detail for troubleshooting. To make life easier, there are also a number of preconfigured queries to help us filter out the noise or simply messages that are not relevant to our situation. We can see these by going into the properties of each query and editing the query statement. Equally, we can create our own status message query by using **Create Status Message Query** from the ribbon and entering our own query or a modified version of another. In the status message viewer, we should pay particular attention to the filter symbol.

This allows us to further filter out any unwanted noise and concentrate on specific components, systems, or messages among other things.

In here we will see status messages that give us some detail into what went wrong. It goes without saying that we would want to take a look at the warning and error messages but also don't forget to align a time against the issue you are troubleshooting. It can be common that people are drawn toward an error while ignoring the time stamp and using that as an explanation only to discover later that it was a red herring. Sometimes the messages in here can become a little cryptic, and this is also on a sliding scale in parallel to the level of detail. With detail often comes confusing messages that need some de-obfuscation before we can understand what it is telling us. To an extent, this comes with practice, but we often find on various IT community based websites that people are sharing their errors and explanations. Unfortunately Microsoft don't always publish a full list of error codes and their true meanings. We will look into specific examples of errors in later chapters, but for now we should be familiar with the tools and what kind of information we are going to get from them.

You may have noticed that we have skipped **Conflicting Records**. We will cover it in a later chapter, but essentially this shows us a list of any conflicting client records where we can manually resolve them if required. We will also take this opportunity to mention the various chart views throughout the console, particularly in the monitoring workspace but also elsewhere such as in the software library. These give us another at-a-glance view of the success of a deployment, distribution, client status, endpoint protection status, and so on. These are particularly useful for the novice Configuration Manager administrator and can also be included in security scopes so that basic checks can be performed before escalating a problem.

Log files

For those who have spent any time trying to troubleshoot Configuration Manager, by now they will probably have noticed that there are lots of log files, in fact at last count there are in excess of 360 across clients and servers. The information we find in these log files is also not the most detailed there is available as there are options to enable more verbose logging for deeper troubleshooting requirements. We can find an exhaustive list in the Microsoft TechNet library at `http://technet.microsoft.com/en-gb/library/hh427342.aspx`.

Client log files

In this section, we are going to run through some of the client log files and indicate what we need to be looking at when troubleshooting a Configuration Manager client. Throughout other chapters, we will come back to specific log files and we will look in more detail, so in this chapter we are going to take an overview.

Let us start with the Windows client install files. We can find these by default in `%windir%\ccmsetup\Logs` and all log files are enabled by default.

`ccmsetup.log`	This is the install wrapper for the MSI, we should be looking at the end of the log for:
	CcmSetup is exiting with return code 0
	If there is something else, then we should look into the `client.msi.log` for further information.
`ccmsetup-ccmeval.log`	This log will contain client status and remediation information during setup.
`ccmrepair.log`	If we ever need to repair our client installation, then this is where we should look to begin with.

`client.msi.log`	The MSI log will contain the most detailed view as it runs through the installation or uninstallation routine as defined in the installer. Look out for the red lines in CMTrace but watch out for red herrings like these:
	Windows Installer installed the product. Product Name: Configuration Manager Client. Product Version: 5.00.7958.1000. Product Language: 1033. Manufacturer: Microsoft Corporation. Installation success or error status: 0.
	This is a successful install with an error status of 0 which is good but because the line contains the word `error` CMTrace will highlight red so don't be put off.

If we are using Linux clients, we will see the following two log files:

`scxcm.log`	The default location for the log file is `/var/opt/microsoft/`.
	This can be changed if required. This file will give us information about the initial installation and also the client operations.
`scxcmprovider.log`	Stored in `/var/opt/microsoft/configmgr/`.
	This is the log file for the CIM service that runs the client and also contains information about the operations of the service.

There are also client logs for Apple Mac OSX clients:

`CCMClient-<date_time>.log`	Found in `/Library/Application Support/Microsoft/CCM/Logs`. This log contains information on client operations for application management, inventory, and error logging.
`CCMAgent-<date_time>.log`	This log will give us log on and log off activity and general computer activity. We can find it in `~/Library/Logs`.
`CCMNotifications-<date_time>.log`	If we want to know about the notifications presented on the client, we can find it in `~/Library/Logs`.
`CCMPrefPane-<date_time>.log`	This file logs anything to do with the Configuration Manager preferences pane and is again found in `~/Library/Logs`.

Now, as Configuration Manager was originally and is predominantly for managing Windows clients, there are lots of log files found in `%windir%\CCM\Logs`. If the client is installed on the same server as a Management Point, however, the client installation path by default will be `%ProgramFiles%\Microsoft Configuration Manager\SMS_CCM\Logs`. Following are some of the common logs you will want to get familiar with for day to day problems:

`AppDiscovery.log`	Used specifically with the application model, this log file shows us activities of the discovery engine that checks to make sure applications are installed successfully.
`AppEnforce.log`	Another file specific to the application model, this shows information about installation routines that are initiated to run.
`CAS.log`	This is the content access service that shows information about the local package cache on the client in `%windir%\ccmcache`.
`CcmEval.log`	This log contains information about the client status evaluations.
`CcmExec.log`	Client activities are logged in here as well as SMS agent host activities.
`CcmMessaging.log`	The client talks to the management point; this log will tell us what those conversations were.
`ContentTransferManager.log`	This is particularly useful as it tells us about the BITS or SMB transfer jobs for the client.
`DataTransferService.log`	This file specifically has information on BITS communication for policy or package access by the client.
`execmgr.log`	Packages and task sequences that run on the client are logged into this file.
`InventoryAgent.log`	Hardware inventory, software inventory, and heartbeat discovery information is logged in here.
`LocationServices.log`	If we want to troubleshoot where a client thinks it is in our Configuration Manager environment, then this is the file to check for which management point, distribution point, and software update points are applicable to the client.
`PolicyAgentProvider.log`	Any policy changes processed by the client are logged in here, so we can see when a change has been made.
`PolicyEvaluator.log`	As the name suggests, this log contains information about evaluation of policies by the Configuration Manager client.

StatusAgent.log	Any status messages that are created by the various client components are in this log file.
UpdatesDeployment.log	This log file contains information about the software update deployment evaluation cycle when it is run. It is very useful for troubleshooting software updates on a client.
WUAHandler.log	When software update scans are started, this file logs the activities involved so that we can check that a software update scan is happening.

There are numerous other log files for the Windows client, and whether we need them will depend on what components we have enabled in our Configuration Manager infrastructure. In the next chapter, we will cover the troubleshooting of clients and we will look in to some more of the log files and what to look for.

Server log files

When referring to server log files, we are talking about the server roles and components that make up Configuration Manager. These log files are also plentiful and detailed, so it is important to know which log files relate to which role to save time and prevent picking out log files at random.

When we are installing a Configuration Manager site onto a server for the first time, there is a standard set of log files that we can check for success or failure outside of the installation console. These log files will be stored on the root of the drive that we are installing Configuration Manager onto.

ConfigMgrPrereq.log	The name gives it away but this one deals with pre-requisite checks and installation activities. We should be looking for the word passed at the end of the relevant lines to indicate a successful pre-requisite check.
ConfigMgrSetup.log	This is the big log file that gives us all the detailed information about how our site installation has ran. A lot of the information in here is just that—information. If we use CMTrace and look out for the red and yellow highlights that will give us a good basis on which to assess the success or failure of the installation.
ConfigMgrSetupWizard.log	As we progress through the installer wizard, the various stages are logged in here.
SMS_BOOTSTRAP.log	We will only see this file if we are installing a secondary site as this is simply the launcher log. The full installation log is available in ConfigMgrSetup.log file again.

`smstsvc.log`	During setup, a temporary service is created for checking connectivity and permissions against the servers we specify. The service is removed afterward and this file logs this process.

Now looking at the roles and components we have mentioned earlier in this chapter, one easy place to figure out which log is related to which component is in the Configuration Manager Service Manager. If we don't wish to keep referring to that, then check out the Microsoft TechNet Library link or the following summary table for the frequent use server log files. These log files are all found on the site server in the default location of `%ProgramFiles%\Microsoft Configuration Manager\Logs`.

`ccm.log`	If you are using client push, then this file is very useful to see what is going on behind the scenes and if each client push was successful or went into the retry pile.
`colleval.log`	When you want to know what happened to your collection, if it has disappeared, has changed, or a new one has appeared, then this is where you should be looking.
`compmon.log`	This will give you a good status report on the various components that are on your site server.
`distmgr.log`	When troubleshooting distributions and package creation, you will find yourself in this log file, which also includes information about compression, delta replication, and general information updates.
`inboxmon.log`	You should be aware that there are a number of inboxes behind the scenes of Configuration Manager that are used for processing specific activities. This log will give you information on the processing that takes place.
`mpcontrol.log`	MPControl is only relevant if you have a management point running on the server; however, as it is a fundamental role, you will want to look in here to see what trouble your management point has been up to.
`offermgr.log`	This log file should tell you all you want to know about deployments that have been created.
`offersum.log`	This log meanwhile deals with the deployment status messages.
`pkgxfermgr.log`	The SMS executive component sends content from a primary site server to a distribution point and this file logs those activities. This can be useful alongside the `distmgr.log` file when troubleshooting content distribution.
`sitecomp.log`	As there are many components throughout the whole site, this log file gives you information about the maintenance of those components.
`sitectrl.log`	Any changes made to site control objects are stored in here.

`sitestat.log`	Always worth a check, this log is about the availability and disk space monitoring for all site systems.
`smsdbmon.log`	If there are any changes to your database you would want to know, this is the log file to check.
`smsexec.log`	This is also worth a check for errors as it shows the processing of all the site server threads.
`SMSProv.log`	As previously mentioned, WMI is behind a lot of Configuration Manager and this file will log any WMI provider access to the site database.

It should be noted at this point that there is also another location on a Configuration Manager server that contains log files, and this is `%ProgramFiles%\Microsoft Configuration Manager\SMS_CCM\Logs`. This folder is essentially the Configuration Manager client log file area on the site server. Some log files which reside on this folder will be discussed in later chapters when we look specifically at the components and roles of Configuration Manager.

As with the client logs, there are a number of other log files available depending on what roles we have installed. We will cover these in a later chapter when we look at troubleshooting specific areas of Configuration Manager, but as an indication there are also logs available for the following roles and components:

- Fallback Status Point
- Management Point
- Software Update Point
- Applications and Packages
- Asset Intelligence
- Backups
- Certificates
- Compliance
- Configuration Manager console
- System Center Endpoint Protection
- Software Metering
- Configuration Manager Migration
- Mobile Device Management
- Operating System Deployment
- Out of Band access
- Remote Control

- Reporting Services Point
- Network Access Protection
- Microsoft Intune Connector
- Configuration Manager Console

Summary

Hopefully, this chapter helped you to understand the different levels of logging and status checking available to us in Configuration Manager. They scale from high-level charts in the console monitoring workspace for the uninitiated or first timer through to the deep low-level logs that can take some time to trawl through. As a general rule, it is recommended to always work through those quick and easy checks and then drill down into the relevant log file afterward. Once we become familiar with the log files, we can then jump straight in and use the various tools listed in *Chapter 1*, *The Configuration Manager Troubleshooting Toolkit*, to figure out what is going on. It would be impossible to list every available error message in this book, so it is advised that we use the standard lists from *Chapter 1*, *The Configuration Manager Troubleshooting Toolkit*, and hit the Web. Try not to get side-tracked by other interpretations and keep the approach logical. It may surely take some time, but there is no black magic, and everything has a solution, otherwise you may have found a bug in the product that can be reported on Microsoft Connect, which is a great resource to check if you think you may have done so. The Configuration Manager product group at Microsoft do read these reports and do fix them, so go ahead and log something. In the next chapter, we will look specifically at troubleshooting Configuration Manager clients. This includes which log files to use, how we can extend them, and what options we have available.

3
Troubleshooting Configuration Manager Clients

In this chapter, you will dig deeper into the Configuration Manager client itself and try to understand what makes up the client and how it works. We will look further at the client log files and see what we should typically expect to be looking at in a working and nonworking installation. Then we will look at the various options available for installing the client as this can be a simple but important step in getting the right configuration for the client to work successfully. Finally, armed with this knowledge, we can then start to understand what the common problems can be with clients and how we can typically resolve these. The sections covered in this chapter are therefore as follows:

- Client installation
- The Configuration Manager client
- Client log files
- Common problems

Client installation

Initially, we will briefly cover a section on installing the client. It seems almost too obvious, but quite often people experience problems with Configuration Manager clients only to later find out they installed it with incorrect parameters. This is particularly pertinent when dealing with HTTPS communication as the addition of certificates into anything often seems to send people into a world of confusion. To recap, we have a number of methods available when installing the Configuration Manager client. Some of the methods are as follows:

- Client push
- Manual installation
- Group policy installation
- Logon script
- Software update point installation
- Client upgrade

Keeping it simple, we have only one installer we can use, but two installation files available. These are CCMSetup.exe and Client.msi. Effectively, CCMSetup.exe calls the Client.msi file during installation, but each method has its own installation parameters and this often causes confusion among Configuration Manager administrators. As it is something we may do often during troubleshooting, let us assume that we are installing the client manually from a command line. In this scenario, we have to use CCMSetup.exe as we are unable to run the Client.msi file directly, and this has a number of installation parameters available.

Installation parameter	Description
/source:<Path>	Choose where you want the installer to download installation files from.
/mp:<Computer>	Specify a management point of your choice. If using HTTPS, you must use a **fully qualified domain name (FQDN)**.
/retry:<Minutes>	Specify a retry interval if the installation file download fails. The default value is 10 minutes.
/noservice	Stops ccmsetup from running as a service so that the credentials of the initiating user are used for the installation file download. This is useful when dealing with failed client installs.
/service	This forces ccmsetup to run as a service.
/uninstall	This is the only supported method for uninstalling the client.

Installation parameter	Description
`/logon`	This tells the installer to stop if it finds an existing client.
`/forcereboot`	This allows you to force a restart if the install requires one, otherwise it will wait for a manual restart before the installation completes.
`/BITSPriority:<Priority>`	This controls the download priority for the installation files when they are coming from an HTTP source. Particularly it is useful when working with slow networks. The options available for this are: **FOREGROUND** **HIGH** **NORMAL** **LOW**
`/downloadtimeout:<Minutes>`	Adjust the time to wait for the installation files download. Default is 1,440 minutes (one day).
`/UsePKICert`	This is necessary when using HTTPS communications. The installer will look for a valid certificate to use otherwise it will fall back to HTTP and a self-signed certificate.
`/NoCRLCheck`	This is particularly useful when installing a client that cannot access a **certificate revocation list (CRL)**. Be aware, however, that this can cause a potential security risk.
`/config:<configuration file>`	This allows you to use a template configuration file for installations. This must be located in `%windir%\ccmsetup` when using `/noservice` and the same location as `CCMSetup.exe` when not. The configuration file should be based on a copy of `<Configuration Manager directory>\bin\<platform>\mobileclienttemplate.tcf`
`/skipprereq:<filename>`	If you prefer to not install some of the prerequisites such as Silverlight, then use this option. This can be useful in a strictly regulated environment.
`/forceinstall`	This will force the client to install, regardless if a previous version is found. This is only applicable for Configuration Manager 2012 SP1 and newer.

Installation parameter	Description
`/ExcludeFeatures:<feature>`	If you want to exclude features of the client such as the Software Center, then this is the parameter for you. The only option available for this in versions up to 1511 is ClientUI.

These parameters are available strictly for installations with the `CCMSetup.exe` installer; however, if we are installing through client push or from a task sequence step, then we do not have exactly the same parameters available. When using either of these two methods, we need to use a whole different set of parameters that are classed as parameters for the `Client.msi` installer specifically. This is quite important to understand as people often fall into the trap of using slash parameters in a task sequence, for example, and then wonder why they don't have the desired client as the task sequence engine simply ignores them.

There are currently 35 published `Client.msi` parameters, and listed as follows are some of the most common and the most useful ones that we might use to get the client configured just how we need it, particularly in a troubleshooting situation. Some of the parameters relate to extended logging features and other settings, which we will cover later in this chapter, and correlate directly to the registry entries that we see.

Installation Parameter	Description
`CCMALWAYSINF=`	If the client is going to be solely an Internet-based client, we must use this during client installation. When we use this, we must also specify the Internet name of the server using the `CCMHOSTNAME` parameter.
`CCMCERTSEL=`	When using HTTPS communication, it can often be confusing which certificate to use where, and there also may be numerous certificates in the store. We can use this option to specify exactly which certificate for the client to use based on the `Subject Name` or `SubjectAlternative Name`.
`CCMCERTSTORE=`	In conjunction with the previous parameter, we can also direct the client to a particular certificate store referenced by the store name.
`CCMHTTPPORT=` and `CCMHTTPSPORT=`	If we are using custom port numbers for our client communication, don't forget we need to reflect this in the client install with either of these parameters.
`SMSCACHESIZE=`	This allows us to specify the size of the client cache in MB. The default value is 5,120 MB.

Installation Parameter	Description
SMSMP=	Management points in a site are effectively chosen at random by the client unless preferred management points are used. If we want the client installer to initially use a specific management point, then we can do so with this parameter. If the management point is configured for HTTPS only, the value must contain `https://<fqdn>` as the value.
SMSSITECODE=	It is often recommended to use this parameter with any installation to ensure that clients are speaking to the correct site. It is especially useful if we are in a multisite hierarchy. Note that we cannot use this parameter in a task sequence step.
CCMADMINS=	This is a lesser used parameter but can be very useful in environments where account privileges are somewhat restricted. Use this option to specify an account or group that can access client settings and policies.
NOTIFYONLY=	If we require the client to only notify of client problems instead of the default remediation that it will attempt, then this is the parameter to use.
CCMENABLELOGGING=	For troubleshooting purposes, we can enable more detailed logging for the client installation by setting this parameter to TRUE. This should not be used for every installation though due to the amount of logging produced.
CCMDEBUGLOGGING=	This parameter extends the standard logging level during client installation by setting the value to 1. It can only be used when CCMENABLELOGGING is set to TRUE.
CCMLOGLEVEL=	This parameter sets the logging level for the Configuration Manager client ranging from a value of 0 to 3. Level 0 is the most verbose and the default is 1.
CCMLOGMAXHISTORY=	This parameter defines how many files are retained once the working log file reaches its size limit. The default is 1 and this file is stored with a `.LO_` extension.
CCMLOGMAXSIZE=	Here we can define the maximum size for log files to reach before a new one is provisioned. The default value for this is 250,000 bytes and the value must be at least 10,000.

Not all parameters have been listed here, but you may have noticed that there are differing options available with `CCMSetup.exe` and `Client.msi`. We can use these together with `CCMSetup.exe` and use the slash parameters followed by the MSI parameters. For example:

```
Ccmsetup.exe /mp:server1.company.ad.local SMSSITECODE=PR1
CCMLOGLEVEL=0
```

To acknowledge the software update install which is also available, we can use all parameters available as this option utilizes the CCMSetup.exe file, but the difference is that the installation is performed via a WSUS server and delivered to the client as with software updates.

A full list of all installation parameters for both CCMSetup.exe and Client.msi is available from the Microsoft TechNet library at http://technet.microsoft.com/en-us/library/mt489016.aspx. The installation process for Apple Mac OSX and Linux clients offers us very little in the way of extended installation parameters, particularly by comparison to the Windows client. For this reason, it is recommended to refer to the Microsoft TechNet library for details on the installation process.

For further information on OSX client installations, refer to: https://technet.microsoft.com/en-gb/library/jj591553.aspx.

For further information on Linux client installations, refer to: https://technet.microsoft.com/en-us/library/jj573939.aspx.

The Configuration Manager client

Before we can start to properly troubleshoot the Configuration Manager client, it is important to understand what the client actually is and does. At the end of the day, we can use all of the tools listed in *Chapter 1*, *The Configuration Manager Troubleshooting Toolkit*, but if we do not fundamentally understand how the software is supposed to work, then we are almost working blindfolded. As with anything, a little knowledge can often go a long way. The Configuration Manager client can be installed on multiple operating systems, which include Windows, Apple Macintosh OSX, and Linux-based operating systems, and each has their own installation media. Proportionate to most implementations, we will concentrate primarily on the Windows client but also take a brief look at the OSX and Linux client.

The file and folder structure of the client is really quite simple. In a Windows client, we have the following three folders that contain all the files required by the agent.

- %windir%\CCM: This is where the client files and all its logs are stored. This folder and its subfolders contain all the necessary system files, executables, and MOF files that run the Configuration Manager client along with the client messaging queues.

- `%windir%\ccmcache`: This is the cache area for software downloads. This folder has a default size of 5,120 MB and can be changed in size during the installation or purged if required when troubleshooting. If we deploy content that is larger than the cache size on the client, then the client will return a `100050` status message, which can be seen in the status messages in the console. Any content stored in the cache folder is available for 24 hours by default, after which point it can be purged by new incoming content. Remember, though, if the content is configured to persist in client cache, then this will remain until the cache is cleared or the size of the cache is increased. A number of subfolders named sequentially are created for each piece of content downloaded, and inside these we can see the actual installation files in their original format once the content has been delivered. This information is of particular relevance when looking into the deployment of packages and applications as we can manipulate the cache during troubleshooting to ensure that you are receiving the content you expect.

> If you are experiencing software installation issues when the content is delivered to the client, it is often worth running a hash check against the content in the client cache and comparing with the original source to ensure that the content has not changed during the delivery mechanism.

- `%windir%\ccmsetup`: This is essentially where the Configuration Manager installation binaries and logs are stored. These can also be used for reinstallation or removal of the client locally if necessary. The `Ccmsetup.log` and `Clientmsi.log` files contained in the logs subfolder will also contain a record of all the installation parameters each time the client is installed and uninstalled up until the point of the maximum log file size. This folder persists on the machine even after a client is removed, so we can use this to check historical installation attempts. We also see that this folder contains numerous individual components and prerequisites of the client such as `SCEPInstall.exe` for System Center Endpoint Protection and `Silverlight.exe` for the Software Center. We can use these to reinstall individual components as required.

When we install the Configuration Manager client, there are a number of registry keys created such as:

- HKEY_LOCAL_MACHINE\SOFTWARE\Microsoft\CCM
- HKEY_LOCAL_MACHINE\SOFTWARE\Microsoft\CCMSetup
- HKEY_LOCAL_MACHINE\SOFTWARE\Microsoft\SMS

Similar to the folders, the CCM registry key contains the majority of client settings, and the CCMSetup registry key contains some information about the installation. Along with storing the client settings, the CCM key gives us lots of useful information, which can help when troubleshooting. There are several subkeys for the various components and the settings of those components are stored accordingly, so it is not advisable to start changing these unless you are confident of the outcome. If we take a look at the CCMEval subkey, we can easily see such pieces of information as which site the client is assigned to, how many times it failed to contact a management point, and the last evaluation time. All of this is useful information when trying to get to the root cause of a problem. The CCM key also contains some global logging information for each component and the respective log file names for each component. All the information in here can be useful when comparing against Configuration Manager policy to ensure that it is applying correctly. The CCMSetup key gives us information such as the last successful installation parameters and the last valid management point, as well as the last state ID—again, all useful information. There is also the SMS key that contains further information about the client and hails from previous versions of Configuration Manager when the product was known as SMS.

The final piece of the Configuration Manager client is the WMI repository. As mentioned in an *Chapter 1, The Configuration Manager Troubleshooting Toolkit*, WMI is common throughout the application as a whole and the following WMI repositories are created during the Configuration Manager client installation:

- Root\CCM
- Root\CIMv2\SMS

Within these WMI repositories are all the client side classes used by Configuration Manager. We will cover some common issues with this a little later in this chapter, but we should be aware of these and know which tools we can use to interrogate them.

Hidden files

In Configuration Manager, there are three hidden files that can be manually created and can control the way the product works. The files are completely empty and will be recognized by either the Configuration Manager client (`ccmexec.exe`) or the server (`smsexec.exe`) process.

- `NO_SMS_ON_DRIVE.SMS`: This is there for servers only, it must be placed on the root of a drive and tells the process to ignore that drive for locating any Configuration Manager files.

- `SKPSWI.DAT`: This file is relevant specifically for Configuration Manager clients and simply tells the process to ignore the folder where this file sits when performing any software inventory. You can use several of these files and also put one of these on the root of a drive in order to skip the whole partition. This can be particularly useful when there are folders that you know do not contain any files you want to inventory and can be used as an exception to the rules set in client policy.

- `ARCHIVE_REPORTS.SMS`: This file should be created on a Configuration Manager client in the `%systemroot%\ccm\inventory\temp` folder and is used to retain copies of all software or hardware inventory scans, whether they be full scan or delta scan. The files are created in an XML format and can be read in whichever XML viewer you choose; however, the folder itself requires elevated privileges, so the application should run elevated. This should only be done on a temporary basis for troubleshooting purposes as all scans from that point on will be stored in the location that over time could create lots of files, which are typically 100 KB and upward for a full inventory. Once this is no longer required, the inventory files that were created should be deleted manually as this will not happen automatically.

Trigger client actions

For those not already familiar, each Configuration Manager client gives us a Control Panel applet that can be used for various manual tasks or overrides including triggering client actions. This can also be started from a command prompt by running the following command:

```
control smscfgrc
```

Each of these client actions can be initiated from here outside of the schedules set in policy, which can be particularly helpful when troubleshooting. In addition to this, each of the actions can be triggered from either a command line or PowerShell, so we have the option to run it from a script, in some kind of automation solution, or simply make remote commands to the client. There are also some further actions available to us. The syntax for doing this is as follows.

The following command line example uses WMIC and will trigger a hardware inventory:

```
WMIC /namespace:\\root\ccm path sms_client CALL TriggerSchedule
"{00000000-0000-0000-0000-000000000001}" /NOINTERACTIVE
```

If we want to perform the command against a remote machine, then use the following and replace the COMPUTERNAME value:

```
WMIC /node:"COMPUTERNAME" /namespace:\\root\ccm path sms_client CALL
TriggerSchedule "{00000000-0000-0000-0000-000000000001}" /NOINTERACTIVE
```

Alternatively, for those that prefer to use PowerShell, we can use the following command:

```
Invoke-WmiMethod -Namespace root\ccm -Class sms_client -Name
TriggerSchedule "{00000000-0000-0000-0000-000000000001}"
```

For remote calls, we can add a –ComputerName value following Invoke-WMIMethod. The TriggerSchedule value at the end is different for each action. Following are the most common IDs which are equivalent to those in the Control Panel applet, but for a full list you should refer to the Configuration Manager Toolkit listed in a previous chapter. Note that some actions may require two triggers.

TriggerSchedule ID	Friendly Name
{00000000-0000-0000-0000-000000000121}	Application deployment evaluation cycle
{00000000-0000-0000-0000-000000000003}	Discovery data collection cycle
{00000000-0000-0000-0000-000000000010}	File collection
{00000000-0000-0000-0000-000000000021}	Machine policy retrieval
{00000000-0000-0000-0000-000000000022}	Machine policy evaluation cycle
{00000000-0000-0000-0000-000000000002}	Software inventory cycle
{00000000-0000-0000-0000-000000000031}	Software metering usage report cycle
{00000000-0000-0000-0000-000000000114}	Software updates deployment evaluation cycle
{00000000-0000-0000-0000-000000000113}	Software updates scan cycle
{00000000-0000-0000-0000-000000000026}	User policy retrieval
{00000000-0000-0000-0000-000000000027}	User policy evaluation cycle
{00000000-0000-0000-0000-000000000032}	Windows installer source list update cycle

Save the command and store the Trigger Schedule IDs into variables with a friendly name for easy running when required.

Apple Mac OSX client

The Apple Mac OSX client and the Linux client are relatively simple and do not have the level of complexity that is apparent in the Windows client. All OSX clients do require a certificate to be enrolled, so troubleshooting for this is cross-platform and there will be a requirement for a certificate enrolment profile, which we will we look into in a later chapter. The client installation files are not provided within the Configuration Manager media and must be downloaded separately from the following location: `https://www.microsoft.com/en-us/download/details.aspx?id=47719`.

One thing to note about the OSX client is that Microsoft bundle four utilities along with the client:

- CMDiagnostics
- CMUninstall
- CMAppUtil
- CMEnroll

These are prepackaged and allow the Configuration Manager administrator to enroll a certificate, convert Apple application packages, uninstall the client, and, most importantly, collect diagnostic information about the client for troubleshooting. This makes the client somewhat simpler to troubleshoot but this is expected due to the relatively limited feature set. The Apple Mac OSX client is installed in the following folder: `/Library/Application Support/Microsoft/CCM`

The log files listed in *Chapter 2*, *Configuration Manager Monitoring Workspace and Log Files*, can be found at: `/Library/Application Support/Microsoft/CCM/Logs`

Unix and Linux clients

The Linux client is available for various flavors of Unix and Linux based operating systems. Fortunately, the installation process and the client are the same throughout each version, and the installation and log files are in the same location across the platforms. The client is installed in `/opt/microsoft/configmgr/bin/ccmexec`.

And the log file can be found in `/var/opt/microsoft/scxcm.log`.

There are limited functions we can perform with the client for troubleshooting, but if we require a manual policy check outside of the schedule, then we can run the following command:

```
/opt/microsoft/configmgr/bin/ccmexec -rs policy
```

For a hardware inventory run, we can run the following command:

```
/opt/microsoft/configmgr/bin/ccmexec -rs hinv
```

If we wish to view the log files, then it is recommended to use something like tail as it is tail reader similar to CMTrace for Windows. Run the following commands:

```
tail -F /var/opt/microsoft/scxcm.log
tail -F /var/opt/microsoft/configmgr/scxcmprovider.log
```

Finally, if we wish to uninstall the client completely, we can do so by running the following command:

```
/opt/microsoft/configmgr/bin/uninstall -c
```

We can also use -p for a partial uninstall leaving the Open Management Infrastructure (OMI) intact or -f for a forced install with no prompts. OMI is an open source management stack originally from Microsoft but used by multiple platforms to provide common management standards between platforms.

Client log files

In an earlier chapter, we went through some of the log files that we should be aware of when troubleshooting our Configuration Manager environment. We will focus now on the Windows client-specific log files and what we can expect to see in them.

As ever, the full list of client-specific log files is available on the Microsoft TechNet library at http://technet.microsoft.com/en-gb/library/hh427342. aspx#BKMK_ClientLogs.

Other chapters will cover the role-specific logs such as distribution points, management point, software update points, and so on. This section relates purely to client-specific activities.

Application management

There are three client log files that we can use for troubleshooting application delivery. To be clear, these only apply to the application model and not to packages. The three client log files are as follows.

- `AppDiscovery.log`: This will deal with the discovery of applications and their deployment types. We should be able to see in the log how the client works through the deployment types in the application and their respective detection methods. Remember this is applicable to both install and uninstall deployments, so we can use this log for both.

  When an application is not discovered, we will see lines in the log file similar to that affect:

  +++ Application not discovered.

  We should use this as a marker to check that the detection method is correct or not.

- `AppEnforce.log`: This simply deals with the installation or enforcement of the deployment types that `AppDiscovery` cannot find on the client. As usual, look out for exit codes in this log file to confirm success or failure of an application and we can then further troubleshoot the application installation by checking an application-specific log file or even the event viewer in some cases. On some occasions, it can be the case that this log file actually does not exist on the client. A common reason for such occurrences can be that the client isn't in a correctly configured boundary, the client has been incorrectly installed, or if in operating system deployment scenarios check that the application is set to install from a task sequence in the properties of the application.

- `AppIntentEval.log`: `AppIntent` is effectively the middleman in this and works with the information from `AppDiscovery` to show what is actually required by the client. Common problems found in this log file can include failures to evaluate policy for applications. This can be rerun using the trigger client actions discussed earlier in this chapter.

If we merge the three logs together with CMTrace, we can see in the example in the following screenshot that the process that is followed using this simple application deployment and how the components work together:

Log Text	Component
Entering ExecQueryAsync for query "select * from CCM_AppDeliveryType where (AppDeliveryTypeId = "ScopeId_6E61F03E-E...	AppDiscovery
Performing detection of app deployment type http://demo-cm01/Reports - Web Application(ScopeId_6E61F03E-E39A-4C...	AppDiscovery
+++ Application NOT Discovered [AppDT Id: ScopeId_6E61F03E-E39A-4C19-B84F-5EB567933EFA/DeploymentType_1a9e8fd...	AppDiscovery
No dependencies for DeploymentType ScopeId_6E61F03E-E39A-4C19-B84F-5EB567933EFA/DeploymentType_1a9e8fd9-d24b...	AppIntentEval
+++ Did not detect app deployment type http://demo-cm01/Reports - Web Application(ScopeId_6E61F03E-E39A-4C-B84...	AppDiscovery
Evaluating Application policies for S-1-5-21-307359223-2356355981-3919538702-1104	AppIntentEval
ScopeId_6E61F03E-E39A-4C19-B84F-5EB567933EFA/DeploymentType_1a9e8fd9-d24b-4e79-ba6f-8eb290cbbea9/1 :- Current ...	AppIntentEval
ScopeId_6E61F03E-E39A-4C19-B84F-5EB567933EFA/Application_ae4df908-2f0d-41b3-a466-03b54b6794b8/4 :- Current State ...	AppIntentEval
ScopeId_6E61F03E-E39A-4C19-B84F-5EB567933EFA/RequiredApplication_ae4df908-2f0d-41b3-a466-03b54b6794b8/4 :- Curre...	AppIntentEval
+++ Starting Install enforcement for App DT "http://demo-cm01/Reports - Web Application" ApplicationDeliveryType - Sco...	AppEnforce
The Install action on AppDT "http://demo-cm01/Reports - Web Application" [ScopeId_6E61F03E-E39A-4C19-B84F-5EB56793...	AppDiscovery
The content path is not specified for DeploymentType ScopeId_6E61F03E-E39A-4C19-B84F-5EB567933EFA/DeploymentTy...	AppEnforce
A user is logged on to the system.	AppEnforce
Performing detection of app deployment type http://demo-cm01/Reports - Web Application(ScopeId_6E61F03E-E39A-4C...	AppEnforce
+++ Application NOT Discovered [AppDT Id: ScopeId_6E61F03E-E39A-4C19-B84F-5EB567933EFA/DeploymentType_1a9e8fd...	AppEnforce
Performing detection of app deployment type http://demo-cm01/Reports - Web Application(ScopeId_6E61F03E-E39A-4C...	AppEnforce
++++++ App enforcement completed (1 seconds) for App DT "http://demo-cm01/Reports - Web Application" [ScopeId_6E...	AppEnforce
+++ Discovered application [AppDT Id: ScopeId_6E61F03E-E39A-4C19-B84F-5EB567933EFA/DeploymentType_1a9e8fd9-d24...	AppEnforce
Entering ExecQueryAsync for query "select * from CCM_AppDeliveryType where (AppDeliveryTypeId = "ScopeId_6E61F03E-E...	AppDiscovery
Performing detection of app deployment type http://demo-cm01/Reports - Web Application(ScopeId_6E61F03E-E39A-4C...	AppDiscovery
+++ Discovered application [AppDT Id: ScopeId_6E61F03E-E39A-4C19-B84F-5EB567933EFA/DeploymentType_1a9e8fd9-d24...	AppDiscovery
+++ Detected app deployment type http://demo-cm01/Reports - Web Application(ScopeId_6E61F03E-E39A-4C19-B84F-5EB...	AppDiscovery
No dependencies for DeploymentType ScopeId_6E61F03E-E39A-4C19-B84F-5EB567933EFA/DeploymentType_1a9e8fd9-d24b...	AppIntentEval
Evaluating Application policies for S-1-5-21-307359223-2356355981-3919538702-1104	AppIntentEval
ScopeId_6E61F03E-E39A-4C19-B84F-5EB567933EFA/DeploymentType_1a9e8fd9-d24b-4e79-ba6f-8eb290cbbea9/1 :- Current ...	AppIntentEval
ScopeId_6E61F03E-E39A-4C19-B84F-5EB567933EFA/Application_ae4df908-2f0d-41b3-a466-03b54b6794b8/4 :- Current State ...	AppIntentEval
ScopeId_6E61F03E-E39A-4C19-B84F-5EB567933EFA/RequiredApplication_ae4df908-2f0d-41b3-a466-03b54b6794b8/4 :- Curre...	AppIntentEval
No dependencies for DeploymentType ScopeId_6E61F03E-E39A-4C19-B84F-5EB567933EFA/DeploymentType_1a9e8fd9-d24b...	AppIntentEval
Evaluating Application policies for S-1-5-21-307359223-2356355981-3919538702-1104	AppIntentEval
ScopeId_6E61F03E-E39A-4C19-B84F-5EB567933EFA/DeploymentType_1a9e8fd9-d24b-4e79-ba6f-8eb290cbbea9/1 :- Current ...	AppIntentEval
ScopeId_6E61F03E-E39A-4C19-B84F-5EB567933EFA/Application_ae4df908-2f0d-41b3-a466-03b54b6794b8/4 :- Current State ...	AppIntentEval
ScopeId_6E61F03E-E39A-4C19-B84F-5EB567933EFA/RequiredApplication_ae4df908-2f0d-41b3-a466-03b54b6794b8/4 :- Curre...	AppIntentEval

A common mistake that can be picked up in these logs is an incorrect detection method on the deployment types in the application. For ease of reading, it is recommended to take advantage of the merge logs feature in CMTrace. This can be done by making a multiple selection of log files with the *Ctrl* key and then selecting the `Merge selected files` checkbox in CMTrace, as shown in the following screenshot:

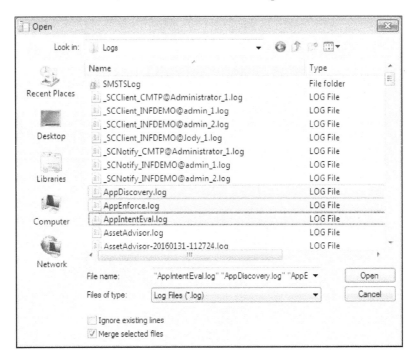

Package delivery

There are a handful of log files that we can check when dealing with package delivery to the client.

- `CAS.log`: This is the log for the content access service and it simply maintains the client cache. It is always worth a quick check for errors to make sure we don't have cache problems. A typical example of a cache error would be that there either isn't enough space available or content cannot be cleared from the client cache. Errors for these symptoms will include the following:

  ```
  Not enough non-active cache to delete
  Not enough space in Cache
  CreateContentRequest failed
  ```

- `ContentTransferManager.log`: This log file shows the creation and running of content transfer manager jobs that are used to transfer content with BITS or SMB. If we filter on the job GUID in CMTrace, we can trace the entire job from creation to completion. Particularly with this log file, we should look out for any suspended jobs that would prevent the deployment from completing. This is identified by the following line in the log file:

  `CTM job {GUID} suspended ContentTransferManager`

  One such example of a reason for this could be that the content is not available on any distribution points that can typically be identified with this line in the log file:

  `CCTMJob::UpdateLocations - Received empty location update for CTM Job`

- `DataTransferService.log`: This log file works hand in hand with the content transfer manager and records all BITS communications for policy or package access. In this log, we want to look out for any failed jobs as we can then link them together with the other log files to see what caused the problem. A typical failed job should light up red in CMTrace with the following line:

  `CDTSJob::JobError : DTS Job ID={GUID}`

- `ExecMgr.log`: Among other things, this log records information about packages or task sequences that are executed by the client. This log file can contain a number of different errors but typically we should look out for program execution errors such as the following:

  `Script for Package:INF0001E, Program: App-v Client failed with exit code 1603`

- This should be highlighted with CMTrace, so should be relatively easy to spot and can be investigated according to the specific exit code:
  `FileBITS.logs`.

Despite the name, this file records package information regarding access with SMB. This can be frequently used to help troubleshoot branchcache deployments that, at times, can be difficult. In that scenario, the log file can contain errors such as the following:

`Failed to check PeerDistribution status. NOT able to do branch cache. BranchCache Is Not Enabled`

It is worth remembering at this point that there is an error lookup facility embedded into CMTrace. This can be used to translate many error codes into something more meaningful. To do this, simply click on **Tools | Error Lookup** or use *Ctrl + L*. Enter the error code and select the **Lookup** button. An example of the output is shown in the following screenshot:

Software Center

Software Center is quite simple in that it really only has one log file specific to the application:

- `SoftwareCenterSystemTasks.log`

This log will give you information about the validation of prerequisites for Software Center to ensure that the application can run. Any errors within this log file will relate to the running of the application itself as opposed to the contents of it such as application or package deployments.

General client activity

There are a number of other log files that are dedicated to running the client itself as opposed to one particular component or activity. These are listed as follows.

Log files	Description
CAS.log	The CAS.log is the log file for the Content Access Service. This includes information around the discovery of distribution points by clients, download sources, and maintenance of the local client cache.
CCMEval.log	This log file shows maintenance of the client installation and logs evaluations of client health activities.
CCMExec.log	This contains information around activity of the SMS Agent Host (the client service) and also the Agent Wakeup Proxy.
CCMMessaging.log	This file shows us information from communication between the client and a management point.
CCMNotificationAgent.log	Again related specifically to client notification, this log file notes activities from the client side of the process.
ClientIDManagerStartup.log	Particularly useful when working with workgroup clients, this log file contains information regarding the client registration process and also generates the unique GUID for the client.
ClientLocation.log	When a client determines which site to assign to, this log file records information regarding this process.
EndpointProtectionAgent.log	As the name suggests, this file relates specifically to Endpoint Protection and the assignment of the relevant policy.
LocationServices.log	When a client is locating management points, distribution points, and software update points, it uses this log file to output the activity from this process.
PolicyAgent.log	Any request for policy for machine or user is logged here. This process also includes using the data transfer service.
StatusAgent.log	Any events created by the agent application itself are logged in this file.
WindowsUpdate.log	As the name suggests, this relates to Windows updates. It contains information from when the client contacts the software update point (WSUS) and whether or not the updates available are applicable to the client. This file is found in the %WINDIR% folder.

These are the core log files that should keep us occupied when looking at client issues in general. Between them we can see which boundary a client is in, which management point and distribution point it is dealing with, any status notifications that are generated, client approvals, and policy-related information. With this information to hand, it should stand us in good stead for picking out where the problem lies.

Extended logging

The Configuration Manager client has certain extended features available that are not necessarily obvious upon first inspection. On occasions, we may find that we need further information than that provided in the log files by default. Fortunately, we can extend the logging into what is referred to as debug logging by using registry edits. Obviously by enabling these features, there will be an increased disk space requirement and a little overhead due to the increased processing requirements, so do bear this in mind. However, on most modern machines, the user may not even notice. We need to run `regedit.exe` elevated as an administrator and browse to the following key: `HKEY_LOCAL_MACHINE\SOFTWARE\Microsoft\CCM\Logging\@GLOBAL`.

From this point in the registry, there are a handful of changes that we can make to enable verbose or in other words more detailed logging on your client.

From this key, we can browse further down the key and change the following values:

- `LogLevel`: By default will be set to `1`. Change this value to `0` to enable verbose logging.
- `LogMaxHistory`: By default will be set to `1`. Change this value to amend how many backup log files to create when the original fills to capacity. We can see these renamed accordingly with the date included in the filename.
- `LogMaxSize`: By default is set to 250,000 (decimal) and designates the size of the log files. This is equivalent to around 244 KB. Set this to the desired size; as an indication, `1048576` will mean 1 MB per log file. The minimum value for this is 10,000, which is just under 10 KB.

An example of how one of these values can be set with PowerShell is as follows.

This can also be done easily with PowerShell by using the following commands:

```
$RegistryPath = "HKLM:\Software\Microsoft\CCM\Logging\@GLOBAL"

$Name = "LogLevel"

$Value = "0"

New-ItemProperty -Path $registryPath -Name $name -Value $value
-PropertyType DWORD -Force | Out-Null
```

This can be easily extended to include other features if required.

These extended attributes can also be set at client installation time using the `CCMSetup.exe` parameters explained earlier in this chapter.

When setting these, don't forget to consider all of them together multiplied by all the log files. Do the math and make sure you don't make things worse by creating a lack of disk space or too much overhead on the machine. It is probably also worth mentioning that we may well find ourselves in a position where we actually want to reduce the amount of logging maybe due to a rogue process or repeating error, for example. We can do so separately simply by reducing the `LogMaxHistory` and `LogMaxSize` values accordingly and restarting the SMS Agent Host (`ccmexec.exe`) service.

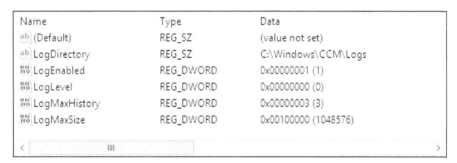

If we do want to increase the logging level, then the last registry change we need to make is to add a new key named `DebugLogging` to the `Logging` key, so we should see the following key: `HKEY_LOCAL_MACHINE\SOFTWARE\Microsoft\CCM\Logging\DebugLogging`.

Under this key, we should create a string value (`REG_SZ`) named `Enabled` and set the value to `True`, as shown in the following screenshot:

Once we have made the required changes, we must restart the SMS Agent Host (`ccmexec.exe`) service, and then we will start to see the verbose logging, which can obviously be helpful in troubleshooting scenarios. If it is not intended to leave this enabled, don't forget to reverse the change to the defaults.

With the compliance settings feature, we can create some configuration items and a configuration baseline to apply these registry settings to our clients in bulk with a suitable collection either permanently or temporarily. Otherwise we can simply have them handy ready for ad hoc troubleshooting situations.

Common problems

It is always difficult writing a book on troubleshooting as there is no way to list every possible error that could be seen and how to resolve it. Particularly in a product such as Configuration Manager that incorporates many dependencies outside of the core applications and is often well distributed, it simply would not be feasible. We can, however, cover some of the more frequently occurring problems and error messages based on both my own and others' experiences with the product.

External factors

First of all, we should get this sometimes obvious hurdle out of the way — external factors. So often it has been seen that outside influences put heed to successful operations where Configuration Manager itself is not actually at fault. Due to the level of logging available in Configuration Manager, people are often led down blind alleys without considering the basics. Can the client actually see the server and vice versa? In these times of increased IT security, we should ensure that communication channels are open and running through the correct ports. Fortunately, Configuration Manager clients generally use fairly standard ports such as TCP 80, 443, 445, 135 for most operations, but if you add in things like WOL, PXE booting, and multicast, then these can sometimes get lost in the midst of firewall rules. The simple way to hit this one is to check the TechNet library for the ports you should be using for your client and then jump into your preferred network monitoring tool to see what is being stopped. The webpage for this can be found at `https://technet.microsoft.com/en-gb/library/hh427328.aspx`.

From previous experience, it is common that network administrators like factual content as it saves them the time and equally they can't argue with it. Another mention along the same lines is DNS. This can cause so many problems in Configuration Manager environments as communication is reliant on good DNS records. The obvious common issue here is using remote tools from the console and the DNS A record for the client is either absent, in multiples so we are in a round robin, or it is simply stale and hasn't been scavenged. If we keep DNS healthy, then the Configuration Manager environment will thank us for it.

Another factor to consider mainly when implementing new or extending a site out is server hardening. In many environments, IT administrators apply security hardening to their server, which in reality is only right and fair. However, when we are installing a new product onto a hardened server, this can often cause failures due to a setting that can often be overlooked or taken for granted as being enabled or disabled. If at all possible, we should install into a clean operating system, by all means apply hardening afterward, and test thoroughly to ensure full operation of the components. Many people have spent many hours trying to understand problems that have been caused by an often minor group policy change.

Windows Management Instrumentation

WMI is considered by many as a bit of a dark art at times, but as we have seen in *Chapter 1*, *The Configuration Manager Troubleshooting Toolkit*, there are various tools available to us to help us work with WMI. A number of tools help us visualize WMI, which can also help in many cases.

We might find lines in the `execmgr.log` file with failed to connect errors followed by a relevant code similar to the following:

```
Failed to open to WMI namespace '\\.\root\ccm' (800xxxxx)
```

This obviously does not read well and would correctly lead us to think that there were WMI issues and after a little searching decide that rebuilding WMI may be an option. Often when we are troubleshooting what seems to be a WMI-related problem, it is an easy option to decide to delete or rebuild the WMI repository, which, in some cases, may be the only option but often is not the right thing to do if we want to get to the bottom of the problem and save time next time, and there is also risk of data loss. If the SQL database had problems, we would seldom just flatten it, so we should really treat this in the same way as it is essentially a mini-database. Check the error code against the WMI error constant list in the TechNet library or even in CMTrace and try to figure out what that could possibly be. The following table is taken from the Microsoft TechNet Library and gives us a good starting point (`https://msdn.microsoft.com/en-us/library/windows/desktop/aa394559.aspx`).

Term	Description
0x80041068 - 0x80041099	Errors that originate in WMI itself.
	A specific WMI operation failed because of:
	An error in the request, for example, a WQL query fails or the account does not have the correct permissions.
	A WMI infrastructure problem, such as incorrect CIM or DCOM registration.

Term	Description
0x8007xxxx	Errors originating in the core operating system. WMI may return this type of error because of an external failure, for example, DCOM security failure.
0x80040xxx	Errors originating in DCOM. For example, the DCOM configuration for operations to a remote computer may be incorrect.
0x8005xxxx	Errors originating from ADSI (Active Directory Service Interfaces) or LDAP (Lightweight Directory Access Protocol), for example, an Active Directory access failure when using the WMI Active Directory providers.

Some of the more common errors seen by Configuration Manager clients are actually not WMI specific but can often be interpreted as such.

- 0x80004005: We are likely to see this error a lot. It is not specific to WMI, however, and unfortunately, it simply means *generic failure*, which obviously is not helpful. To get further information is dependent on where we see this error displayed. We should identify the more specific log files related to that component or process and start to obtain further information that way. For example, if this is in operating system deployment, then we can reference the SMSTS.log. It may be that this is related to a client installation and we refer to the CCMSetup.log or the Clientmsi.log.

- 0x80070005: Remember this one as we will also see this at some point. It translates to Access Denied.

- 0x800706BA: This code basically means that it cannot see the client on the network and it translates to RPC_S_SERVER_UNAVAILABLE. Check out the firewalls and ports for this one.

- 0x80041002: WBEM_E_NOT_FOUND: This requires a little more investigation with other information to put it in the right context.

- 0x8004100E: Like the previous step, this requires researching with some background information but translates as WBEM_E_INVALID_NAMESPACE.

Another alternative option to rebuilding the WMI repository suggested by Microsoft is to recompile the MOF files.

For more information on how to decide whether or not a repository is corrupt or not, refer to this blog article from Microsoft to help make a decision: https://blogs.technet.microsoft.com/askperf/2014/08/08/wmi-repository-corruption-or-not/.

MOF files are the files that contain the class definitions used in WMI. If we jump into the initial site server installation log file `ConfigMgrSetup.log`, we see various references to MOF files being compiled. It is recommended, however, that we do some further reading with the aforementioned article on this if we are going to attempt it to ensure that we do not create any further problems. We can also compare the WMI repository against a known working machine that should be the same and see if any of the classes are missing. There are also a number of WMI hotfixes released by Microsoft, so it is worth checking these out with the error codes to see if the problem actually has a software bug, which can be patched. It is also worth mentioning that we should always have the latest available patches available where possible, and should a ticket ever be raised with Microsoft support, one of the first questions asked will be if the environment is running on the latest available cumulative update.

Background Intelligent Transfer Service

BITS, as it is more commonly known, can often require some investigation as it is widely used in Configuration Manager to get content from A to B. There are various options available in client policy to throttle BITS at certain times of the day for certain clients and to certain speeds. Then there is the fact that sometimes BITS can seemingly fail us altogether and not actually deliver the expected content to the client. All of these things are not completely unheard of, so we should know how to approach them. Firstly, it is suggested that we work our way through the aforementioned log files to ensure that content delivery is being processed correctly and should actually be taking place before diving into the details. As BITS is not unique to Configuration Manager (it was introduced in Windows XP for software update delivery), it has a dedicated admin tool called `BITSAdmin.exe`. This can be run from a command prompt and has a whole host of available parameters. As usual, for the full list of options, check the Microsoft TechNet library at `http://msdn.microsoft.com/en-us/library/aa362813.aspx`.

Previously `BITSAdmin` was the go to tool and still has some validity but it is actually now a deprecated tool and in more recent times Microsoft introduced PowerShell cmdlets to replace this.

Cmdlet	Description
`Add-BitsFile`	This allows to you add files into an existing BITS job.
`Complete-BitsTransfer`	Self-explanatory really, it allows you to complete a BITS transfer job.
`Get-BitsTransfer`	You will likely use this the most to simply view what jobs currently exist.
`Remove-BitsTransfer`	This cancels a BITS transfer job.
`Resume-BitsTransfer`	This resumes a BITS transfer job from suspension.

Cmdlet	Description
`Set-BitsTransfer`	This is another particularly useful cmdlet as it allows you to modify a BITS transfer job.
`Start-BitsTransfer`	You can create a new BITS transfer job if required.
`Suspend-BitsTransfer`	You can suspend a BITS job that can be useful when there are multiple jobs and you want to troubleshoot just one.

Also do not forget that we can query each cmdlet further by adding `-?` at the end.

Certificates

If we are running Configuration Manager systems in HTTPS mode, then the likelihood is that we will have already been through the pain and have a good measure of what to do in problem situations. For those new to HTTPS, it more often than not is a slow start while we figure out why a client isn't speaking to a management point and which certificate you should have where. Fear not though, the key to success is not to overcomplicate matters. When using HTTPS in Configuration Manager, it still fundamentally works in the same way, just with the addition of a few certificates to secure the communications. It is probably a fair estimate that around 80 percent of certificate-related problems are because the client has the wrong certificate. So, first and foremost check and double-check that the client has the correct certificate. We can do this by following these steps:

1. Open up the **Microsoft Management Console** (`mmc.exe`).
2. Add a snap-in by selecting **File** | **Add/Remove Snap-in...**.
3. Select **Certificates** from the list on the left and click on **Add**.
4. Choose **Computer Account**, and then click on **Next**.
5. Choose the applicable computer, click on **Finish**, and then click on **OK**.
6. Browse to the **Personal Store**.

If we have nothing at all, then there is a problem straight away. Assuming we do have a certificate, we need to check a number of things.

Issued To	Issued By	Expiratio...	Intended Purposes	Certificate Template
DEMO-WIN81.infdemo.com	infdemo-DEMO-DC01-CA	23/02/2016	Client Authentication	ConfigMgr Client Domain Joined

- Has the certificate expired?
- Is the certificate based on the correct certificate template?
- Has the certificate been enrolled correctly?

- Is the certificate path complete?
- Does the certificate have the correct Subject name or Subject Alternative Name?

In the preceding example screenshot, the certificate is for a domain joined machine, and usually this would be delivered by a group policy; therefore, once we have that right, we can just about rule out the template, the enrolment, and the certificate path. If we are managing workgroup machines, then we will have had to enroll the certificate either manually or with a script that will supply the name in the request; check this for typos and again check the template used.

The definitive list for certificate requirements is on the Microsoft TechNet library at `http://technet.microsoft.com/en-us/library/gg699362.aspx`.

So, for the remaining 20 percent of certificate-related problems, we have a few options:

- Ensure that we have the correct client installation parameters in place.
- Check out the relevant log file.
- Test the client for a response from the management points with the management point test URLs (`https://servername.domain.com/SMS_MP/.sms_aut?mpcert`).

  It may be required to import the client certificate into the browser in order to obtain a successful return but this URL will list the management point certificate and verify that the client can read this. A typical output from this should return something like this:

  ```
  <?xml version="1.0"?>
  -<MPCertificate>
  <Certificate>308202…</Certificate>
  </MPCertificate>
  ```

- The `https://servername.domain.com/SMS_MP/.sms_aut?mplist` URL, again it may be required to import the client certificate into the browser in order to obtain a successful return but this URL will confirm that the client can successfully communicate with the management point. A typical output from this should return something like the following:

  ```
  <?xml version="1.0"?>.
  -<MPList>
  -<MP FQDN="DEMO-CM1511.infdemo.com" Name="DEMO-CM1511.INFDEMO.COM">
  <Version>8325</Version>
  -<Capabilities SchemaVersion="1.0">
  <Property Name="SSLState" Value="0"/>
  </Capabilities>
  </MP>
  </MPList>
  ```

- Compare certificates against a known working machine.

- Consider any other external factors such as load balancers, routers, or WAN optimizers.

- Use the HTTP error codes discussed in *Chapter 1, The Configuration Manager Troubleshooting Toolkit*.

Between all of the options listed, we should be able to get to the bottom of the problem. Don't get caught up in the confusion that often comes with certificates and keep it simple.

Summary

Clients by nature of the product are really the biggest component of Configuration Manager by the typical ratio of clients to site system, so probability says that we are most likely to hit problems in this area. There is a lot of information available from the Configuration Manager client, so choose wisely before jumping in. Using the information provided, isolate the problem and we can extend the logging if we need further information. Once we have narrowed down where the problem lies, use the right tool for the job and check against the standard error codes provided. As with any troubleshooting, we should take a logical approach and, above all, write it down, blog it, or share it, so that next time it comes up we have a head start.

In the next chapter, we will look into the top levels of a Configuration Manager installation by seeing what we can do to troubleshoot hierarchies of sites, the site servers themselves, and the technologies that hold them together.

4

Troubleshooting Hierarchies and Site Servers

In this chapter, we will take a look at the major components of the Configuration Manager infrastructure, which are the servers that make up a Configuration Manager hierarchy. We will consider how to troubleshoot a hierarchy of sites from the **Central Administration Site** (**CAS**) through the Primary Site and Secondary Site and how these work together so that we can start to troubleshoot. Another fundamental component of the Configuration Manager environment includes Microsoft SQL Server, so it is only right and correct that we should at least know our way around some basic troubleshooting skills with this and know what to look out for as this really is a large piece of the underlying technology in Configuration Manager these days. Finally, we will delve into the Configuration Manager console and also where Configuration Manager and Active Directory meet. Active Directory is fundamental to the Configuration Manager installation, and while we can manage machines outside of this, we will need to know where to look when things go wrong. Equally, the console might seem like almost a minor component but again it is fundamental to working with Configuration Manager even with the advent of PowerShell cmdlets. We will take a look at how to fix this and also how it can help us fix other aspects of the Configuration Manager hierarchy. So to summarize, this chapter comprises the following topics:

- Hierarchies and Site Servers
- SQL Server
- The Configuration Manager console
- Active Directory

Hierarchies and Site Servers

Let us start with a quick summary of the hierarchy of Configuration Manager sites. A multiple site hierarchy is now used less and less in implementations due to advancements in Configuration Manager 2012 and current branch versions. This is because site roles and components are becoming more highly available and can be designed in such a way that negates the requirement for multiple sites. The vast majority of sites that are installed now are a single primary site. However, we cannot ignore or exclude the multiple site hierarchies that will exist and how we can troubleshoot such hierarchies. We will not go into the details of why you should or should not have multiple sites—that debate is for another book.

There are three levels in a Configuration Manager hierarchy and in its simplest form it can consist of a **Central Administration Site**, a **Primary Site**, and a **Secondary Site**.

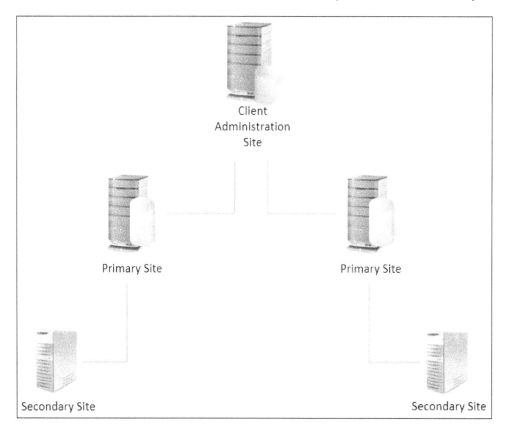

It is quite likely that if we use multiple sites in an organization, then we will have multiple primary sites or a primary with multiple secondary sites. Each level of the hierarchy requires its own database, the secondary sites commonly run from Microsoft SQL Express, and this is automatically installed if a SQL Server instance is not available. Because the sites are part of a hierarchy, as you would expect, there are a certain amount of data that flows between the sites, which includes database information and files. This process is referred to as replication and is one of the most common areas of troubleshooting when it comes to a multiple site infrastructure. Now, there are several ways to troubleshoot this, again, going from high level in the monitoring workspace through to the status messages and then into the detail of the logs.

In the monitoring workspace, we have the **Site Hierarchy** diagram that gives us a great high-level view of the hierarchy. In the following example screenshot, there is just a CAS and a primary site with an issue showing for the site replication:

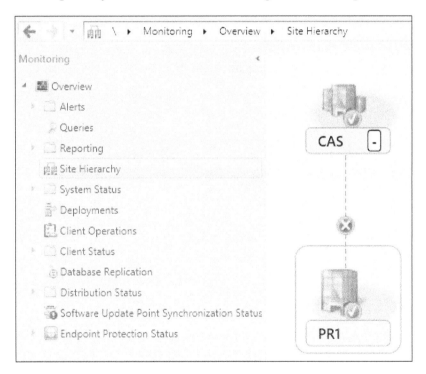

This is the first place to see the status of the site and its relationships to other sites including a health indicator. For those who are at all familiar with Microsoft System Center Operations Manager, this view is quite similar to a typical dashboard view that we may see in a management pack in the Operations Manager console. This view allows us to hover and right-click over each site and site link to get a quick look at the health state, and this indicator is based on the number of status messages for each category of error, warning, or OK. We can also link into the status messages for that particular site. The site hierarchy diagram also gives us the option to **Configure View Settings** from the ribbon and add a physical location for the sites that we can then see in the geographical view, which again can be seen by hitting the ribbon option. These options combined give us a good high-level view of the entire site hierarchy with options to dive a little deeper.

Replication

There are two types of intersite replication in Configuration Manager: SQL replication and file-based replication. Within those two replication methods, there are three main data types, each containing different pieces of information.

Microsoft has provided the following table that accurately outlines what kind of data is replicated, what data type it is categorized as, and which replication type is used.

Data type	Examples	Replication type	Where is data found?
Global data	Collection rules, package metadata, software update metadata, Deployments	SQL	CAS, all primary sites, secondary sites (a subset of global data is replicated here)
Site data	Collection members, HINV, alert messages	SQL	CAS, originating primary site
Content	Software package installation bits, software updates, boot images	File based	Primary sites, secondary sites, distribution points

The preceding table is taken from the following Microsoft blog post that does a great job of explaining an overview of replication in Configuration Manager: `http://blogs.technet.com/b/server-cloud/archive/2012/03/06/data-replication-in-system-center-2012-configuration-manager.aspx`.

It is probably worth mentioning at this stage that the replication used by Configuration Manager is not the native replication used by the Microsoft SQL server. So if you are adept at working with Microsoft SQL, don't expect to necessarily jump right in here to find out what is going on as we have to use the Configuration Manager console, at least initially, anyway. So now that we have a grasp of how replication works and what is replicated, we can start to troubleshoot appropriately and focus on the relevant area.

If we take a look in the monitoring workspace, we will see the **Database Replication** view. Please note that for those that are in a flat hierarchy (that is, single primary site), this will be completely empty. If we are in a multiple site hierarchy, however, then we will see a summary view of the database replication between our sites. If we have multiple sites, we will see multiple entries.

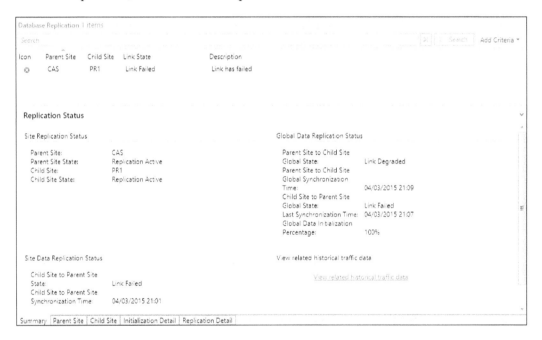

From this console view, we have various options available on the ribbon, the right-click menu, and the split pane tabs at the bottom of the window. A run-through of the tabs shows us a configuration overview and status for both the parent and child site in that particular part of the hierarchy. We will also see the **Initialization Detail** tab that shows us each replication group complete with status and also which data type each group belongs to. The final tab in this view gives us some really good information about **Replication Detail**, which again lists all the replication groups but most importantly lists the last send time and receive time for replication from both the parent and child site. We can also see synchronization intervals in minutes, so this should be fairly easy to work out if one of our replication groups has not been running or has missed a cycle, if that hasn't already been figured out. Overall, these give really great information, particularly for a console window that often restricts us just to the high-level detail.

Now, that is the tabs covered. Let us take a look at the ribbon and right-click options — they are the same:

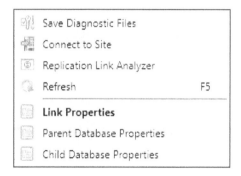

The first available option sounds like the kind of thing we might want when troubleshooting — **Save Diagnostic Files**. Select this option and we will be asked to save a comma separated variable (CSV) file that contains a summary including the last synchronization time and general status of the parent to child link and an overview of the parent and child site with details including certificates used and firewall rules. To be brutally honest here, the diagnostics file is all well and good, but it doesn't really give us an awful lot of useful information that we couldn't have already found out from the console. This brings us onto the next item, **Replication Link Analyzer**, which can also be run from a command line using this executable:

```
%ProgramFiles(x86)%\Microsoft Configuration Manager\AdminConsole\bin\
Microsoft.ConfigurationManager.ReplicationLinkAnalyzer.Wizard.exe
```

Again, this is quite self-explanatory in its function, but when we select this, it runs a live job to analyze the link on the site relationship that is selected. The link state will be one of the following three states:

- Active
- Link Degraded
- Link Failed

The result of running the **Replication Link Analyzer** is an option to read the resulting log and an option for a report. The report gives a nice mid-level `.htm` report, which is easy on the eye.

 A note to make, though, is that during testing for the purposes of this chapter, the CAS server was deliberately halted to create a failed link. This could also be caused by losing access between the site SQL servers through TCP port `1433` or `4022` for SQL replication.

When running this report, all was showing well in the report, which is obviously not correct. It took around 10 minutes in the lab environment to actually show the link as failed as opposed to degraded as this is based on a cumulative error counter. If we want to see any level of detail, then the log file is the place to go as usual. The log file to use for this is `ReplicationLinkAnalysis.log`, which is available from the **Replication Link Analyzer** but is also automatically stored on the desktop. In here, we will see line-by-line descriptive checks being made and we can simply look out for the lines marked with an error. Even better, use CMTrace to read the log file, but, as usual, beware of any red herrings as there are lines that check for items such as the SQL error log file location. As we read through the log, we will see that the **Replication Link Analyser** actually does quite a few checks and will make some suggestions to us in the console based on those findings. If we read the log, we will find the following checks being performed:

- Is the SMS service running?
- Is the SMS Replication Configuration Monitor component running?
- Are the ports required for SQL replication enabled?
- Is the SQL version supported?
- Is the network link available between the two sites?
- Is there enough space for the SQL Database?

- Does SQL Server service configuration exist?

- Does an SQL Server Broker service certificate exist?

- Are there any known errors in SQL log files?

- Are the replication queues disabled?

- Are the server times in sync?

- Is the transmission of data stuck?

- Does a key conflict exist?

Based upon the results of these checks, we may be offered a suggestion by the Replication Link Analyzer. For example:

```
"Replication Link Analyzer recommends restarting the MSSQLSERVER service
on SERVER-CAS.DOMAIN.LOCAL"
```

Followed by an option to restart the service for us, it is also worth mentioning that any such errors are automatically reported as alerts in the Configuration Manager console through the alerts we discussed in a previous chapter. What we can do, however, is reduce the time limit for those alerts by selecting the **Link Properties** item from the ribbon or right-click menu. We then see that we can reduce the default time of 30 minutes before Configuration Manager creates an alert and we can also reduce the number of retries before the link is set to degraded (default 12) and ultimately failed (default 24). It is recommended to reduce all of these limits for a typical environment so that, at least, we get to know what is happening in Configuration Manager replication and we can choose to ignore it or adjust to our preferences. With the default limits, we could be sitting not knowing that something is going wrong behind the scenes. It is generally better to know that something has happened even if it is no longer an issue.

Besides the Replication Link Analyzer, there are not a lot of options for troubleshooting replication issues. There are manual checks we can perform but these are just about the same tasks as the Replication Link Analyzer will carry out for us. This whole concept was somewhat of an upheaval from previous versions of Configuration Manager where the process was much more manual as the replication mechanism was quite different to recent versions of the product. The information given to us by a combination of the console and the Replication Link Analyzer is quite substantial for most troubleshooting tasks, particularly when compared to other areas of the Configuration Manager console monitoring workspace.

Log files

The vast majority of replication problems can be at least diagnosed if not solved through the console options, but if we want or need to take it that step further, of course, there are some log files associated with site replication. We have already covered the log file from the Replication Link Analyzer, but there are two other log files that we can look into for information about Configuration Manager replication:

- `rcmctrl.log`
- `replmgr.log`

These log files can be found in the default location of `%ProgramFiles%\Microsoft Configuration Manager\Logs`, but obviously each path may differ slightly depending on the install location. Just like the enhanced logging we discussed when troubleshooting clients, there is also an enhanced troubleshooting tweak available for these logs too. Again this can be activated by way of registry edit, so the usual warnings apply and suitable precautions should be taken before making any changes to the registry. If you edit the following registry value:

- `HKEY_LOCAL_MACHINE\Software\Microsoft\SMS\Components\SMS_ REPLICATION_CONFIGURATION_MONITOR\Verbose logging`

The default value is `0`, which is the standard logging level and we have the option to increase this to:

Value	Log Level
0	Errors and key messages
1	Above + warnings and more general information
2	Verbose or full logging

The `ReplMgr.log` file will give us some information about the replication of files between the site server components and the scheduler component of Configuration Manager. A typical example could be as shown in the following screenshot:

Scanning high priority outbound replication directory.	SMS_REPLICATION_MANAGER
Did not find any replication files.	SMS_REPLICATION_MANAGER
Scanning normal priority outbound replication directory.	SMS_REPLICATION_MANAGER
Found 1 replication files	SMS_REPLICATION_MANAGER
There may be more replication files coming in, wait 5 seconds and scan again.	SMS_REPLICATION_MANAGER
Did not find any additional replication files.	SMS_REPLICATION_MANAGER
Scanning low priority outbound replication directory.	SMS_REPLICATION_MANAGER
Did not find any additional replication files.	SMS_REPLICATION_MANAGER
Minijob created. Priority 2, transfer root (\\BOOK-CAS.demo.local\SMS_CAS\inboxes\replmgr.box\ready\2_i8dpea.PR1).	SMS_REPLICATION_MANAGER
Waiting for outbound replication files...	SMS_REPLICATION_MANAGER

This is not the most informative of logs but it does give us an idea of what is happening with replication.

The `Rcmctrl.log` file is really where the majority of logging takes place as it records the activities of database replication between sites in the hierarchy. When we enable the verbose logging option in particular, we can expect to see a significant amount of line-by-line activity that is, as always, best viewed with CMTrace in order to get any highlighted errors. Again, don't forget we can merge these two log files together to get a continuous stream of the site to site replication logs as they come in but don't forget to use the pause function.

SQL Server

Microsoft SQL Server is at the core of Configuration Manager, even more so now than in previous versions of the product. Therefore, it goes without saying that we need to ensure that the database server and services remain healthy at all times in order to keep our Configuration Manager environment running smoothly. We will cover some best practices in a later chapter; however, as usual, it is worthwhile knowing your way around Microsoft SQL Server if you are a Configuration Manager administrator. It should be noted right away that Configuration Manager has a very strict policy on database and instance **collation,** which should always be set to `SQL_Latin1_General_CP1_CI_AS`. Any other collation is not supported and can create unpredictable results in our Configuration Manager installation. To change this, generally would require a reinstallation of SQL Server; there are exceptions but this is usually the easier option. Let us take a look at some of the other common factors that can cause problems with the database behind Configuration Manager.

SQL performance

Configuration Manager is not particularly a database-intensive product on the whole, especially when you compare to some of the other Microsoft System Center products such as Operations Manager or Service Manager. That said, if our SQL server is running slowly, then we will see this impact on both the performance of the console and the performance of the product overall. Don't forget that if we are in a multiple site hierarchy, then we will have several SQL instances across various servers, so we should really check them all or at least make a logical troubleshooting path from one site to another. Generally speaking, there are two main areas of bottle neck for SQL servers: memory and disk I/O. CPU can also become a third bottle neck; however, this would normally only be noticeable in much larger primary site installations. Configuration Manager is no exception to this, and there are Microsoft recommended limits for minimum memory values assigned to SQL server depending on the hierarchy. This is quite easy to check though using something like Task Manager, Resource Monitor or better still Performance Monitor. It is recommended that we check the average disk queue length to make sure it is not high: a consistent value of more than around 2 is generally considered undesirable. If the memory in our SQL server is reaching the heights of 90 percent usage we may need to investigate which processes are using this and if it is SQL Server then we can investigate further and potentially make changes to the maximum memory. As a guide to what amount of memory the SQL instance should be allocated, Microsoft provides figures of around 50-80 percent of the system memory for a co-located SQL instance and around 80-90 percent of the system memory if using a dedicated server. If we want to set a maximum memory value for an SQL instance, then we can open SQL Server Management Studio and run a simple T-SQL command.

For example, if the server is co-located with the site server and contains 16 GB RAM:

```
16GB = 16384MB
75% of this  = 12288MB
```

Execute the following command to set the value:

```
EXEC sys.sp_configure 'max server memory (MB)', '12288'; RECONFIGURE;
```

We need to then restart the SQL service to complete the process, but be warned that this will close any open connections.

We can perform a good level of troubleshooting of the SQL server using the built-in windows application **Performance Monitor** (`perfmon.exe`). As a guide, a good set of counters to add to the data collector set should include at least the following:

Counter Category	Counter Name(s)
Paging file	`% Usage _Total`
Processor	`% Processor Time _Total`
Memory	Available Mbytes
Thread	All relevant `smsexec` and `sqlservr` instances
Physical/logical disk	Avg. Disk sec/Read
	Avg. Disk Bytes/Read
	Avg. Disk sec/Write
	Avg. Disk Bytes/Write
	Avg. Disk Queue Length
Process (sqlservr.exe)	`%Processor Time`
	`%Privileged Time`

There are obviously many more counters available and these may be more relevant depending on the specific situation. There are lots and lots of guides out there for how best to monitor SQL. This is not intended to be an in-depth guide into SQL server, so it is recommended that you converse with the database administrator responsible for the Configuration Manager instance. One very obvious option, however, would be to implement the SQL Server Management pack for System Center Operations Manager should this be an option. This provides us with a high level of information and combined with the management pack for Configuration Manager it is a very useful tool for troubleshooting any site server.

At this point, we should refer to yet another Microsoft article that dives deep into the finer details of finding SQL blocks and deadlocks in Configuration Manager. This can be a common cause of delays in any SQL instance and this article explains very well how this can impact a Configuration Manager installation:

```
http://blogs.technet.com/b/configurationmgr/archive/2014/12/16/
troubleshooting-configmgr-2012-using-extended-events-to-find-blocks-
in-sql-server.aspx
```

Finally, for this section, SQL Indexing is something that can have a huge effect on the performance of a Configuration Manager environment, and this becomes most noticeable when browsing with the Configuration Manager console. It can make a huge difference to an application working from a nonindexed database to a well indexed one. It is highly recommended that the Configuration Manager maintenance task **Rebuild Indexes** is always enabled and scheduled to run at least once a week. This task, however, is known to be somewhat inefficient and can be unreliable at times. It is therefore also recommended to either run the indexing script manually or introduce a completely separate indexing method for the Configuration Manager database. The script used by the rebuild indexes maintenance task is as follows:

```
SELECT DISTINCT sch.name + '.' + Object_name(stat.object_id),
                ind.name,
                CONVERT(INT, stat.avg_fragmentation_in_percent)
FROM    sys.Dm_db_index_physical_stats(Db_id(), NULL, NULL, NULL,
'LIMITED') stat
    JOIN sys.indexes ind
      ON stat.object_id = ind.object_id
         AND stat.index_id = ind.index_id
    JOIN sys.objects obj
      ON obj.object_id = stat.object_id
    JOIN sys.schemas sch
      ON obj.schema_id = sch.schema_id
WHERE   ind.name IS NOT NULL
    AND stat.avg_fragmentation_in_percent > 10.0
    AND ind.type > 0
ORDER   BY CONVERT(INT, stat.avg_fragmentation_in_percent) DESC
EXEC Sp_msforeachtable
  @command1="print '?' DBCC DBREINDEX ('?', ' ', 80)"
```

This script can be ran manually in SQL Server Management Studio or as part of an SQL maintenance plan to ensure that the indexing is performed. Everything before the EXEC statement can be ran separately to list all the tables with a greater than 10 percent level of fragmentation. If we run the whole statement including the EXEC, this will reindex the relevant tables.

There are also other methods of indexing SQL that are well regarded in the Configuration Manager and indeed SQL world. One such example can be found in a Microsoft blog post at http://blogs.technet.com/b/smartinez/archive/2014/03/28/talking-database-in-configmgr.aspx.

SQL logs

SQL, of course, has its own logging capabilities and we should know where to go when troubleshooting your Configuration Manager SQL instance.

The default location for Microsoft SQL error logs is: `%ProgramFiles%\Microsoft SQL Server\MSSQL.n\MSSQL\LOG\ERRORLOG`.

Each install location may be different if the install drive is nondefault and the `.n` in the path represents the version number. For those using SQL Server 2012, for example, this will be 11 and SQL Server 2014 will be 12.

We will also find that SQL uses the **Application Log** of the Event Viewer to log various errors. It is always worth taking a look in here as usually the alerting is quite verbose and meaningful even for the non-DBA.

SQL trace and extended events

Finally, we have the SQL profiler, which, for the uninitiated, is similar to a network monitor but specifically for seeing the queries and requests being made within the SQL server. Running SQL profiler has a performance impact on the SQL server therefore the person responsible for that server should be aware of any profiling activity being performed on the server. Using the profiler does put an overhead on the SQL server but equally shows us all the queries and executions being performed in the SQL database, which can be very useful when troubleshooting a specific issue. This is really a last resort for troubleshooting SQL issues for Configuration Manager specifically and it should only really be performed by someone who knows how to do it. For that reason, we will not cover this process in detail but suffice to say there is information out there that can help with this.

In recent years, another technology called **Extended Events** has become a popular option as an alternative to SQL Trace due to the reduced overhead on the SQL instance. We are not going to cover this in any detail but we should be aware that this can be an option for troubleshooting. As the name suggests, Extended Events allows us to synchronously generate event data on specific events that we feel are relevant to the problem we are investigating. There is lots of information out there regarding Extended Events, but as a good place to start, refer to the Microsoft TechNet article at: `https://msdn.microsoft.com/en-us/library/bb630282(v=sql.120).aspx`.

You should always remember to apply the correct antimalware exceptions to all servers. Recommended exceptions lists are available at `http://social.technet.microsoft.com/wiki/contents/articles/953.microsoft-anti-virus-exclusion-list.aspx`.

The Configuration Manager console

It seemed only right that we should give the Configuration Manager console a mention as, regardless of PowerShell, it is still the most widely used method of accessing the product. There is a little bit of troubleshooting we can do for the console itself, but further than this we can use the console to troubleshoot other aspects of our Configuration Manager site at a deeper level.

Troubleshooting the console

Some people may not realize that the Configuration Manager console is a 32 bit application; therefore, we won't find it in the same place as our site installation when we are looking for log files. The default installation location for your console is in the Program Files (x86) folder:

- 64 bit OS: `%ProgramFiles(X86)%\Microsoft Configuration Manager\AdminConsole`.

- 32 bit OS: `%ProgramFiles%\Microsoft Configuration Manager\AdminConsole`.

In this folder, we will see the `AdminUILog` folder that contains the available log files for Configuration Manager:

- `AdminUI.ExtensionInstaller.log`
- `CMSitePSProvider.log`
- `CreateTSMedia.log`
- `FeatureExtensionInstaller.log`
- `SMSAdminUI.log`

The names are fairly self-explanatory here but the logs will give us the troubleshooting information we will need about console extensions, task sequence media creation, and console errors among other things. Probably the two most frequently used of these log files would be `CreateTSMedia.log` and `SMSAdminUI.log`. The former will give us any failure information about the creation of task sequence media because this is done directly from the console as the logged on user, and the latter will give us information about the actual console application itself. If we see console crashes, then this will be logged in `SMSAdminUI.log`, and these crash reports commonly reference the HTTP and WMI codes, which we have already discussed in an earlier chapter.

Probably the most common problem with a console is the failure to connect to the Configuration Manager site. Besides role-based access, this relies on the SMS provider being available to provide access to the SQL server from the console. If there are multiple SMS providers in an installation of Configuration Manager, we should ensure that these are available, otherwise some console connection may fail should the SMS provider be offline or otherwise. Another common issue around this can be the blocking of ports by a firewall between the console and the SMS provider. These should also be checked to make sure they are available. The ports required from a console to an SMS provider are identified by Microsoft as the following:

Description	UDP	TCP
RPC Endpoint Mapper	135	135
RPC	N/A	Dynamic/Ephemeral ports Typically 49152-65535

Debug modes

With the Configuration Manager console, there are several options available to enter an enhanced view of the console and the content within it. This can be really useful not only for troubleshooting console access but also if we want to get extra information about packages, applications, OS images, and so on. There are several console parameters we can use to execute the console in these enhanced modes:

- Debug view
- Namespace view
- Reset settings
- Ignore extensions
- No restore

To enter these modes, we need to add an extension to the executable, for example:
```
%ProgramFiles(X86)%\Microsoft Configuration Manager\AdminConsole\bin\
Microsoft.ConfigurationManagement.exe /sms:debugview=1.
```

The full list of available parameters is given in the following table:

Option	Description
`/sms:debugview=1`	A debug view is included where applicable and the debug view shows raw content properties such as names and values.
`/sms:NamespaceView=1`	This shows a namespace view in the console.
`/sms:ResetSettings`	The console ignores any user persisted connection and view states.
`/sms:IgnoreExtensions`	This disables any console extensions such as the ever popular right-click tools.
`/sms:NoRestore`	The console ignores any previously persisted node navigation.

In the following screenshot, we will see that the console has been started with the debug view enabled. This gives us a **Tools** workspace to use where we can drill down into specific WMI classes and see relevant properties. This can be useful as we can get real-time detailed information relevant to particular content as there is also an additional right-click option that will show object details and jump into the Tools workspace. If we are having problems deploying a specific application, package, or operating system, for example, then this can really help. In fact, some Configuration Manager administrators use this particular console parameter permanently:

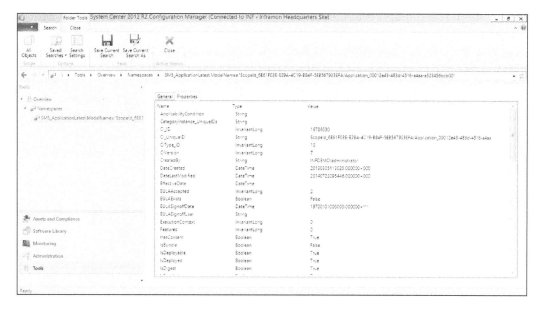

It is recommended to try the rest of the console parameters as they are often forgotten but can be really useful when working at a lower level on a particular problem.

 Why not create multiple shortcuts for the Configuration Manager console each with the console parameter specified in the target. Then they are always there when you need them.

Active Directory

Active Directory plays a major part in the successful operation of our Configuration Manager sites, so it is important that we know where the touch points are and how these can affect the smooth running of Configuration Manager. We are not going to dive deep into Active Directory as the borders can get blurry as to where we need to troubleshoot, but let us look at a few of the clear relationships with your Active Directory.

Schema extension

We will first take a brief look at the Active Directory schema extension for Configuration Manager. The purpose of this is to allow Configuration Manager to have information about many Configuration Manager features and components available from contacting their Active Directory, which is a known good source of information. It is not absolutely necessary, but is recommended and is applied in the vast majority of Configuration Manager environments. There are a few ways of applying the schema extension, and the most common is probably the `ExtAdSch.exe` executable from the Configuration Manager installation media. When we run this, it creates a log file named `ExtAdSch.log` on the root of the `C:\` drive on the machine it was ran from. This will typically contain a list of all the classes and attributes that were added to the Active Directory schema. If we don't have the luxury of that file or are unsure if the schema is updated, then we can check using the Windows tool **ADSI Edit**. If we start this and connect to the Schema like so, then we will see a list of all available Active Directory Schema:

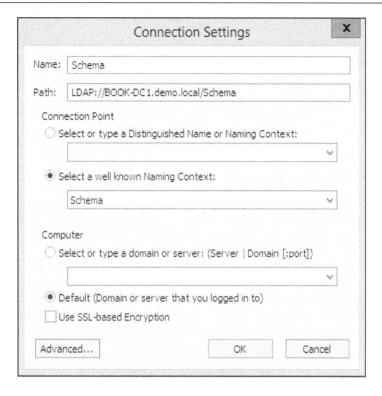

If we then check this list, we should see each of the following attributes and classes:

Attributes

The following is the list of available attributes:

- cn=mS-SMS-Assignment-Site-Code
- cn=mS-SMS-Capabilities
- cn=MS-SMS-Default-MP
- cn=mS-SMS-Device-Management-Point
- cn=mS-SMS-Health-State
- cn=MS-SMS-MP-Address
- cn=MS-SMS-MP-Name
- cn=MS-SMS-Ranged-IP-High
- cn=MS-SMS-Ranged-IP-Low
- cn=MS-SMS-Roaming-Boundaries
- cn=MS-SMS-Site-Boundaries

- `cn=MS-SMS-Site-Code`
- `cn=mS-SMS-Source-Forest`
- `cn=mS-SMS-Version`

Classes

The following is the list of available classes:

- `cn=MS-SMS-Management-Point`
- `cn=MS-SMS-Roaming-Boundary-Range`
- `cn=MS-SMS-Server-Locator-Point`
- `cn=MS-SMS-Site`

Although not strictly a schema extension, there is also the **Systems Management** container associated with this which can be easily checked to ensure that it is present and the permissions are correct. The container does not replicate across domains; therefore, the container should be created in each domain where there clients will reside. We should ensure that the relevant site server has **Full Control** permission on the container, which also applies to **This object and all child objects**.

If we find that any of the schema extensions or the container is missing, we can quite easily recreate these with minimal impact using ADSI Edit, but, as usual, we should always make recovery plans as necessary.

DNS and DHCP

The **Domain Name System** (**DNS**) should get a mention as without this life as a Configuration Manager administrator would be so much more difficult. It is always worthwhile keeping DNS healthy as Configuration Manager will primarily rely on this to make connections out to clients, clients to servers, and simple day-to-day tasks such as making remote control and **Remote Desktop Protocol** (**RDP**) connections. Although there are mechanisms within the product that will also attempt to use IP addresses, DNS is generally used as the first port of call. Things to look out for include the following:

- Stale records, that is, not scavenged from DNS
- Static records that are incorrect
- Multiple records, particularly if a client has multiple network adapters
- Failed zone replication between DNS servers

Again this is not a deep dive into Active Directory or DNS, but we should be aware of the potential implications of badly maintained DNS.

DHCP also requires a mention as this can actually update our DNS and so has an equally import role to play in maintaining a healthy Configuration Manager. DHCP is also generally well utilized in operating system deployment, so we should ensure that this is fully functioning at all times. Each environment can be different; however, we need to ensure that any IP Helpers or DHCP options specified are maintained and updated.

Certificate services

If we are running our Configuration Manager site with at least some HTTPS roles enabled, then we are quite likely to be using **Active Directory Certificate Services**. After years of working with this product, this is the area that never fails to catch people out. There are some quite obvious checks to make such as ensuring that our **public key infrastructure (PKI)** is up and running and that all certificates are not expired or revoked, as well as having the appropriate certificate chains in place on the appropriate clients and servers.

The common place people seem to trip up on this is getting the certificate templates configured correctly in the first place. Microsoft has created an excellent blog post for our perusal, which is definitely worth checking against to make sure the fundamental parts are present and correct.

```
http://blogs.technet.com/b/configmgrdogs/archive/2015/01/22/
configmgr-2012-r2-certificate-requirements-and-https-configuration.
aspx
```

Once we have our template created, we should ensure that we are enrolling the certificates correctly. If these are Active Directory clients, then ensure that an auto-enrolment group policy exists and is functioning properly; this can be checked by running a GPResult /R or RSoP command from a command prompt or PowerShell window. We can also force the application of group policy by using a gpupdate /force command once any required changes have been made. If we are dealing with workgroup-based machines, this is where there is a greater scope for error as we must supply the name of the client in the certificate request. Check and double-check this as simple typos can stop the whole process in its tracks. If we are using certificates on server roles such as management points, then ensure that we are choosing the correct certificate in the bindings for the appropriate website. Also, using the knowledge gained from *Chapter 3, Troubleshooting Configuration Manager Clients*, makes certain that we have the correct combination of certificate and client install parameters. Make sure a CRL is accessible if this is enabled and don't forget this won't necessarily be available for Internet-based clients.

From previous experience of many long-standing Configuration Manager folk, the fault almost certainly lies with the certificate itself. The chances are we are not using the Certificate Authority explicitly for Configuration Manager, so if the problem is with the certificate provider, then we are likely to see a much more widespread problem in our infrastructure.

Discovery

Another commonly used feature in Configuration Manager is Active Directory based discoveries whether that be for systems, users, groups, or forests. There are a few easy checks we can do to ensure that your discoveries are running as expected. The typical symptom for a nonfunctioning discovery would be that resource records are not appearing in the Configuration Manager console. The first and most obvious check is to make sure that the Active Directory containers and Organizational Units are still present in both Active Directory and the discovery properties; again check for typos or name changes too. It is also worth checking that the machine, user, or group is actually in the container or organizational unit we are expecting it to be in.

Assuming we have made all the basic, common sense checks, we do have some log files available to us which will give a deeper insight into all the discoveries:

Log Name	Description
adsgdis.log	This records Active Directory Security Group Discovery actions.
adsysdis.log	This records Active Directory System Discovery actions.
adusrdis.log	This records Active Directory User Discovery actions.
ADForestDisc.Log	This records Active Directory Forest Discovery actions.
ddm.log	This records activities of the discovery data manager.
netdisc.log	This records Network Discovery actions.

These log files will typically give information about discovery failures such as binding to containers or organizational units or insufficient privileges for a forest discovery account. The errors that we will find in here again conform to the types of error code lists we have already discussed in *Chapter 1, The Configuration Manager Troubleshooting Toolkit*, but on the whole, the content is quite verbose, thus making troubleshooting of discovery relatively painless.

Site boundaries

We couldn't let the subject of Active Directory pass without at least a brief mention of site boundaries. Boundaries are quite fundamental to the primary functions of Configuration Manager in order for the client to know where to obtain content from and/or which site it should be assigned to. It is beneficial to include a reminder that if our boundaries are based upon Active Directory sites, then don't forget that if these are not maintained, we may start to see strange goings on in our Configuration Manager environment. Typical symptoms could include the following:

- Clients not downloading content for installation
- Machines failing operating system deployment
- Clients in the wrong site
- Inconsistent problems with content downloads

It is a good general rule to try not to overlap boundaries where possible. For example, if we have a boundary group based on an Active Directory site with distribution point *A* assigned and another boundary group based on an IP subnet that is included in the Active Directory site but with distribution point *B* assigned, then we can see unpredictable results. Although this situation described for content location is a supported configuration, we should be aware of the possible outcomes. To add to this, an unsupported scenario would be the same situation when used for site assignment as opposed to content location.

There are several types of boundaries available, and it should be noted that the order of preference from highest to lowest should generally be as follows:

- Active Directory Site
- IP Subnet
- IPv6 Prefix
- IP address range

This is because the impact on SQL server can be increased due to the way the boundary types are queried. It should also be acknowledged that the more the boundaries, the higher the theoretical impact on SQL server performance. This is more of a design consideration but should also be observed for troubleshooting.

The moral of the story is really to make all checks and to consider this information before spending time trawling through log files.

Summary

To summarize, what we have seen in this chapter is that the vast majority of multiple site troubleshooting can be performed right there in the Configuration Manager console. There is a considerable depth of information available without having to dive deep into log files or other areas. That said, however, there are still a number of log files available to confirm those suspicions. Don't forget we can also add those parameters to the console for our day-to-day troubleshooting tasks. We have also looked at some of the surrounding technology and systems that contribute to the running of Configuration Manager. We don't need to be an expert in these complementary systems but a little can go a long way and this is not the right book to teach about SQL or Active Directory in detail.

Moving on to the next chapter, we will look further into the specific troubleshooting options available to us when looking specifically at Management points and Distribution points. These are really the two most essential roles in Configuration Manager and, as could be expected, they can occasionally go wrong from time to time. Fortunately, there are a number of methods and practices available to use when troubleshooting them.

5
Troubleshooting Management Points and Distribution Points

In this chapter, we will look at what are really the two fundamental Configuration Manager roles in our site. With the exception of a Central Administration Site, all the other site hierarchies will have at least one management point and one distribution point. Therefore, we should know what to do if and when one of these roles is not working to full effect. There are a number of different configurations and options available when configuring each role, so we will take a look into some of these and how to specifically troubleshoot such variations. As with everything before and after this chapter, a little knowledge can go a long way, so we will spend a little time trying to further our understanding of how each role works. So let us get to it as we have a lot to cover, as listed in the following:

- How a management point works
- Testing our management point
- Troubleshooting our management point
- Management point common issues
- How a distribution point works
- Troubleshooting our distribution point
- Distribution point common issues

How a management point works

As always, if we understand the workings of what we are troubleshooting, we will inevitably reach a solution sooner. Being such an important piece of the Configuration Manager architecture, many people may think that the management point is a large and complex piece of software. Large it is not, complex maybe, but I guess that is subjective. The management point is in simple terms a small web application that the clients will contact to receive service location information, policy information, and also send configuration data to. The management point can be configured in either HTTP or HTTPS mode depending on the implementation and management points can be mixed across an environment. It is important to remember that when troubleshooting any management points configured for HTTPS, the role functions in just the same way as an added layer of security. Often people can be overcome with the fact that there are certificates involved and miss the basic functions. In some circumstances, it can be beneficial to remove any certificates and make the server temporarily HTTP only for the cause of problems to become clear; however, this is not always possible.

The site system role runs in **Internet Information Services (IIS)** on the management point server, and there are also a number of prerequisites that must be in place prior to installing the role. This can sometimes be confusing when installing a new management, and the prerequisites should be double-checked against Microsoft TechNet which is available at `https://technet.microsoft.com/en-us/library/gg682077.aspx#BKMK_SiteSystemRolePrereqs`.

Traditionally, a management point was available for any client to communicate with as long as it was within the same site and online. In fact, this was the native behavior that a client would use for any management point in the site. There is a caveat to this in that there is an order of preference when a client chooses a management point, which is as follows:

- If the management point is HTTPS enabled
- If the management point is in the same Active Directory forest
- Randomly within the same site

This is true traditionally and still is to some extent in the current version. However, since Configuration Manager 2012 R2 Cumulative update 3, we have been able to add some more control into which management point a client communicates with. This update added **Management Point Affinity** which allows us to amend the registry of a client and fix that client to a management point. The registry keys to set this are these:

```
Key: HKEY_LOCAL_MACHINE\SOFTWARE\Microsoft\CCM:AllowedMPs
Type: Reg_Multi_SZ
Value Data: <Server1.domain.com>
```

There are some caveats to this that we should be aware of, and further information on this can be found in this Microsoft blog article available at `http://blogs.technet.com/b/jchalfant/archive/2014/09/22/management-point-affinity-added-in-configmgr-2012-r2-cu3.aspx`.

In more recent versions of the product since Configuration Manager 2012 SP2/R2 SP1, this function was developed further and we now have the facility of **Preferred Management Points**. These are controlled by the use of boundary groups where we can add in a management point and make the clients within that boundary group use that management point as a first preference. There are again some caveats to that behavior which we should be aware of and which can be found in this article available at: `http://blogs.technet.com/b/senthilkumar/archive/2015/08/10/configmgr2012-sp2-r2sp1-preferred-management-points-configuration-and-secondary-sites.aspx`.

Whichever way the management points are configured for use in the site, we should be mindful when troubleshooting that there are now multiple options available. One other point to note is that management points can also use what is known as a **Management Point Replica**, which means that the management point has a replicated copy of the site database, which is closer to the server, and often it is on the same server. If this configuration is in place, then we should be familiar with how this is configured within SQL and be mindful of the differences from a standard management point. This is slightly out of the scope of this book as the vast majority of configuration required for this is performed with SQL, but Microsoft provides a useful guide on how to set this up, move a replica, and uninstall a replica. The guide is available at: `https://technet.microsoft.com/en-gb/library/hh846234.aspx`.

Now to dive a little deeper into the management point itself, if we take a look at IIS on our management point server, then we will see in the `Default Website` that we have an application for `SMS_MP` and `SMS_MP_WindowsAuth`. Don't be fooled though, if we hit explore on these web applications, we will be taken to an empty folder, which by default is `%ProgramFiles%\SMS_CCM\SMS_MP`. However, if we take a look at the **Handler Mappings** feature of the web application, we can see that there are handler mappings, which are listed as follows:

SMS_MP		
Name	**Path**	**Executable**
AboMapperCustom-01234	`*.sms_pol`	`c:\program files\sms_ccm\getpolicy.dll`
AboMapperCustom-01234	`*.sms_aut`	`c:\program files\sms_ccm\getauth.dll`
AboMapperCustom-01234	`*.sms_dcm`	`c:\program files\sms_ccm\getsdmpackage.dll`
ISAPI-dll	`*.dll`	N/A
OPTIONSVerbHandler	`*`	N/A
TRACEVerbHandler	`*`	N/A

SMS_MP_WindowsAuth		
Name	**Path**	**Executable**
AboMapperCustom-01234	`*.sms_pol`	`c:\program files\sms_ccm\getpolicy.dll`
ISAPI-dll	`*.dll`	N/A
OPTIONSVerbHandler	`*`	N/A
TRACEVerbHandler	`*`	N/A

The `AboMapperCustom` numbers will differ in each environment.

We will see that the `AboMapperCustom` handlers map to `dll` files that relate specifically to the function they provide, and this is where the complexity comes into play. If we were to use our favorite network monitoring tool from the troubleshooting toolkit in *Chapter 1, The Configuration Manager Troubleshooting Toolkit*, we would see various requests from our client to the management point referencing the paths listed.

If we look at the firewall ports required for a management point, we see that the management point communicates to the Active Directory Domain Controller, the Configuration Manager site server, and the Configuration Manager database. Logic says that we need to ensure that good communication routes are available from the management point to each component, and this can be a common issue, particularly when implementing new servers.

Testing our management point

So now that we know what the management point actually is, what it does, and what makes up the management point, we can start to troubleshoot effectively. Probably the most well-known method of testing management point communication is to use the test URLs.

To test management point availability, use the following link from a web browser:

```
http://<MP name>/sms_mp/.sms_aut?mplist
```

This should return something similar to the following XML if your management point is functioning and contactable:

```
- <MPList>
- <MP Name="DEMO-CM01.DOMAIN.COM" FQDN="DEMO-CM01.DOMAIN.com">
<Version>7958</Version>
- <Capabilities SchemaVersion="1.0">
<Property Name="SSLState" Value="0" />
</Capabilities>
</MP>
</MPList>
```

The preceding URL will list all available management points in our site with information about their `SSLState`, which as we can see in the example is `0` for HTTP and will be `1` for HTTPS. The test URL verifies to you that the management point is reachable by the client. This query will use the `getauth.dll` file we identified in the last table and sometimes we can see errors in the logs related to this which can often be linked back to WMI error codes we have discussed previously.

To test that a client can successfully view the management point certificate, use the following link from a web browser: `http://<MP name>/sms_mp/.sms_aut?mpcert`.

This should return something similar to this XML if the management point is functioning and reachable:

```
- <MPCertificate>
<Certificate>308202E7308201CF...</Certificate>
</MPCertificate>
```

The certificate value will obviously differ but, again, this will validate that we can see the certificate successfully. Again, as we will see from the previous table, this query will resolve to `getauth.dll`, which again can appear in our log files.

If we are using HTTPS on our management point, we will need to use HTTPS in the URL accordingly. We should also be mindful of having certificates available in the web browser in case a client certificate needs importing as it can be common that there are policies that prevent this. Don't forget the Configuration Manager troubleshooting toolkit from *Chapter 1, The Configuration Manager Troubleshooting Toolkit*, either. In the Configuration Manager Support Center, we can use the troubleshooting tab to run these tests for us automatically with a graphical user interface to make the process easy.

Troubleshooting our management point

When troubleshooting the management point, we have several options available to us, which can range from high-level overview to low-level detail. Let us take a look at where and how we can troubleshoot the management point in Configuration Manager.

Console

It is worth a brief mention of where to look in the console at the Monitoring workspace. The path we will need to navigate is **Overview** | **System Status** | **Site Status**.

Icon	Status	Site System	Site System Role	Storage Object	Total	Site Code
🔘	OK	\\DEMO-CM01.infdemo.com	Management point	\\DEMO-CM01.INFDEMO.COM\C$\Program Files\Microsoft Configuration Manager	0 Bytes	INF

In here, we will see that the management point is listed as a site system role with a high-level color indicator similar to those we have discussed in previous chapters. From here, we can right-click and show messages, reset error counts, and also start the Configuration Manager Service Manager. As always, this is a great starting point that we can use to dig deeper through the status messages and gradually down into the logs or further.

One other easy method of troubleshooting our management point is to enable the option to generate an alert when the management point is not healthy. This is simply a tick box within the properties of the management point and will generate an alert in the console, which can be linked to an e-mail address to inform us immediately if Configuration Manager detects the role as unhealthy.

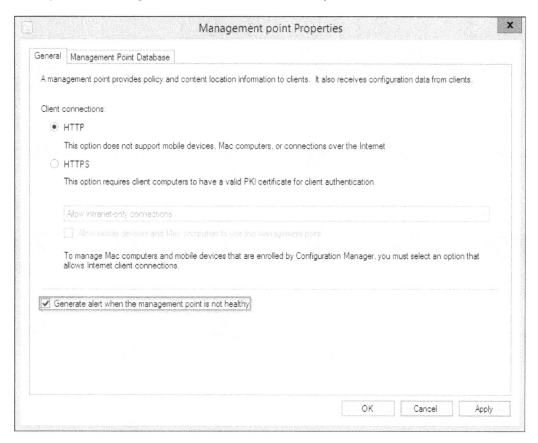

HTTP codes

As the management point is a web application, all standard HTTP and IIS troubleshooting applies. If we run the test URLs and find that we are presented with an HTTP error code, then we can use this as our basis for troubleshooting. If we want more detailed information on that HTTP error code, it is recommended that we run the same test URL on the server itself as this will present us with further information on the HTTP error. We can then use this error code and apply some of our understanding of how the management point works to look up standard HTTP codes and apply this to Configuration Manager. There is always scope for using an Internet search engine as we generally find that the scope of these errors is reasonably limited and it is highly likely that this has been experienced and shared previously. Some of the common HTTP error codes we may experience are identified in the following table:

HTTP Error Code	Definition	Possible issue
500	Internal Server Error	This is quite generic and means that an unexpected condition was encountered. Time to hit the logs for this one.
400	Bad Request	This generally means the request was malformed in some way. Try the request from several clients and see if the results are the same, if so, we have management point issues. If it is a single client, we should check other client activities and troubleshoot the client itself.
401	Unauthorized	A 401 response generally means an authentication-related error. It could be missing or bad authentication.
403	Forbidden	This error is post authentication and therefore means that there is most likely a permissions-related problem after any authentication has occurred between the client and the web application.
404	Not Found	This means that the management point web server did not find the file referenced within the URL. If this is a standard client activity, then the first check is that other clients can perform the same activity against the management point. If there are still 404 responses, then we should check first that the web application exists and check for the files' existence using the aforementioned tables, and then troubleshoot from there.

Log files

There are a several log files which are specific to troubleshooting the management point in its various configurations:

Log file	Description
`%ProgramFiles%\SMS_CCM\Logs\CcmIsapi.log`	All clients messaging from the endpoint is stored in this file.
`%ProgramFiles%\SMS_CCM\Logs\MP_CliReg.log`	A reasonably common occurrence can be troubleshooting client registration activity. This file records all processing activity for client registration on the management point.
`%ProgramFiles%\SMS_CCM\Logs\MP_Ddr.log`	All `XML.ddr` records from clients are converted and copied to the site server and this log file records that activity.
`%ProgramFiles%\SMS_CCM\Logs\MP_Framework.log`	This will give you the fundamental activities of the management point including the client framework components.
`%ProgramFiles%\SMS_CCM\Logs\MP_GetAuth.log`	As the name would suggest, this logs client authorizations.
`%ProgramFiles%\SMS_CCM\Logs\MP_GetPolicy.log`	This file will give you information about policy requests from clients.
`%ProgramFiles%\SMS_CCM\Logs\MP_Hinv.log`	This file records details of the conversions of hardware inventory records in XML from the clients.
`%ProgramFiles%\SMS_CCM\Logs\MP_Location.log`	This file contains location requests from clients and the replies.
`%ProgramFiles%\SMS_CCM\Logs\MP_OOBMgr.log`	If you are using out of band, then this file will contain one-time password activity information.
`%ProgramFiles%\SMS_CCM\Logs\MP_Policy.log`	Communication of client policy is recorded in this log file.
`%ProgramFiles%\SMS_CCM\Logs\MP_Relay.log`	This file stores information about the transfer of files that are collected from a client.
`%ProgramFiles%\SMS_CCM\Logs\MP_Retry.log`	Any hardware inventory retry attempts are stored in this log file.
`%ProgramFiles%\SMS_CCM\Logs\MP_Sinv.log`	This file records details of the conversions of software inventory records in XML from the clients.
`%ProgramFiles%\SMS_CCM\Logs\MP_SinvCollFile.log`	Any files that are collected from the client are recorded in this log file.
`%ProgramFiles%\SMS_CCM\Logs\MP_Status.log`	This file records details of the conversions of status message files (`XML.svf`) from the clients.

Log file	Description
`%ProgramFiles%\Microsoft Configuration Manager\Logs\ mpcontrol.log`	This log file can see frequent use when troubleshooting. It records the status of the management point every 10 minutes. Also, if you have WINS, this file shows the registration of the management point in WINS. This is stored on the site server itself.
`%ProgramFiles%\Microsoft Configuration Manager\Logs\ mpfdm.log`	This file records the action of moving client files to the relevant inboxes on the site server.
`%ProgramFiles%\Microsoft Configuration Manager\Logs\ mpMSI.log`	When you are installing your management point, you can use this log file for detailed information about the MSI installation. This is stored on the site server.
`%ProgramFiles%\Microsoft Configuration Manager\Logs\ MPSetup.log`	This is another file for reference during the installation of the management point; this records activity of the installation wrapper and will give you an overall status for the installation. This is stored on the site server.

Management point common issues

There can be various problems seen with management points in Configuration Manager; however, there are always some that have been seen before and will no doubt be seen again. In the following, we will look at some of the most frequently occurring issues that generally have common resolutions.

Installation

Starting with the installation of a management point, a particularly common issue seen in existing environments is attempting to install a management point on a server that has currently or has previously had a Configuration Manager client installed. This will always fail the installation, and often the reason can be that automatic installation of clients for all discovered computers is enabled in the Configuration Manager site. This normally results in an installer `1603` exit code and a number of `failed to compile` messages in the `MPMSI.log`. However, simply removing the client does not solve this as some WMI classes are still retained on the machine where the client once was. There is an old utility called `ccmclean.exe`, which was intended for previous versions of Configuration Manager, which often can resolve this problem.

Sometimes this does not fully install all traces of the client, so another option is to clear any traces of CCM from WMI with the following PowerShell command:

```
Get-WMIObject -namespace "root" -query "SELECT * FROM __Namespace where
name = 'ccm'" | remove-wmiobject
```

Another problem to be aware of is installing a management point onto a security hardened server. Invariably applying roles to a prehardened server is something to avoid if possible. A commonly seen security policy that can prevent a successful installation of roles, not exclusively management points, is the following:

Network access: Remotely accessible registry paths and subpaths

If this policy is restrictive, then the installation can fail to complete as it attempts to write the following registry key and subkeys:

```
HKEY_LOCAL_MACHINE\SOFTWARE\Microsoft\SMS\COMPONENTS\SMS_EXECUTIVE\
Threads
```

Prerequisites

Along the same lines is to ensure that we have all the prerequisites installed. This sounds quite obvious but it can often be the case of a failed installation. We can find the full list of prerequisites for every role on the Microsoft TechNet website and there are even community tools out there that will install or correct these for you. To check the full list of operating system prerequisites, refer to `https://technet.microsoft.com/en-us/library/gg682077.aspx`.

Another prerequisite to bear in mind, which generally can be overlooked, is the management point connection account. This can be particularly troublesome when the management point is located in a different domain to that of the SQL Server and especially when that domain is untrusted. Bear this in mind prior to a management point installation and factor it into any design when extending a Configuration Manager infrastructure.

Ports and firewalls

There are also a number of port requirements for the management point, as mentioned earlier in this chapter. These can differ depending on various factors, including where in the network the server is, if it is in a trusted or untrusted domain or workgroup, and whether or not it is using PKI certificates. Often forgotten is the access to the Microsoft SQL database, especially if we are using a nonstandard port or named instance for SQL server as these will use a port other than the standard for a default instance, which is TCP 1433. For reference, all the port requirements are supplied by Microsoft on the following web page and this includes which ports, which direction the ports need opening in, and which ports are configurable or nonconfigurable.

```
https://technet.microsoft.com/en-gb/library/hh427328.aspx
```

We must remember that if a management point is in a different network location than the database or primary site server, we must also allow for access to the domain controller for authentication, especially if Kerberos authentication is required.

Certificates

As management points can be enabled in either HTTP or HTTPS mode, any HTTPS communication adds a certain level of complication to matters. The most common occurrence of such an issue is when **Internet-based client management (IBCM)** is enabled. By far, the most common issue using HTTPS enabled roles is certificates. From experience with many HTTPS-enabled environments and also using native mode in Configuration Manager 2007, it could be said that as high as 80-90 percent of management point or client to management point communication issues are down to certificate-related problems. There are a number of steps that must be carried out to ensure we have the correct certificate template, correct certificate in the correct place, and even that it has been enrolled correctly. The key is to remember to validate the templates against Microsoft TechNet and remember that the basic functionality of the management point does not change; it is just the communication that is secured. Microsoft has put together a nice little blog article to help get IBCM setup correctly:

```
http://blogs.technet.com/b/jchalfant/archive/2015/04/15/
prerequisites-for-ibcm-in-configuration-manager.aspx
```

Use of certificates in a Configuration Manager site can also be applied internally as well as over the Internet. The concepts are very similar and we need to ensure that both the management server and the client have the correct certificate and they are enrolled in the correct way. Should the correct certificates not be available on either the management point server or the client, then we will start to see authentication errors in the status messages and the `mpcontrol.log` file. We can begin to troubleshoot these according to the HTTP error code using the lists available from *Chapter 1, The Configuration Manager Troubleshooting Toolkit*. However, generally, we would see a `403 Forbidden` error. This can be checked using the test URL, and if we check this on the management point machines itself, we will get more detailed information to troubleshoot with. Generally speaking though, the first step would normally be to double-check the certificate properties, the certificate template, and the certificate chain

How a distribution point works

Like the management point, the distribution point is a fundamental role in Configuration Manager. The distribution point is a basic requirement of any Configuration Manager installation if we want to deliver software to clients, perform **operating system deployment (OSD)**, install patches, and so on. As always, an understanding of the concepts of a distribution point will serve us well not just in troubleshooting but also in general usage of the product. In a similar way to the management point, the distribution point is essentially a small web application that clients can query for access to content such as an application to install. The difference with a distribution point is that there are variants of the role, which include a pull distribution point and a cloud distribution point. A distribution point can also provide additional functions such as **Preboot Execution Environment (PXE)** services, multicast, and content validation. Let us not forget the primary function of the distribution point which is essentially to provide a cache of installation media for applications and updates using the content library to provide single instance storage for these files. To begin, we will look at the core functionality of the role and what we can do to troubleshoot the distribution point.

When we look at the web application in IIS, we see in the **Default Website** that we have two applications named `SMS_DP_SMSPKG$` and `SMS_DP_SMSSIG$`. As these applications run on IIS, we should be aware that certain file extensions are blocked by default. This being the case, we may need to amend the request filtering in IIS for the `SMS_DP_SMSPKG$` application to include any necessary file extensions. While this is relatively rare, we should be aware of its existence.

The SMS_DP_SMSPKG$ application refers to the SCCMContentLib folder on the drive selected when installing the distribution point. This folder also holds an administrative share of SCCMContentLib$. If the name hasn't given it away yet, this is the content library that was introduced in 2012 versions of Configuration Manager. Within this folder, there are the following three subfolders that make up the content library:

- DataLib
- FileLib
- PkgLib

These are the folders that essentially contain the content that we distributed to the distribution point. The PkgLib folder contains a list of the content available on that distribution point and some information for where to find that in the DataLib folder. The DataLib folder contains information about the content that is held in the distributed manner such as the size, file, last modified time, and, importantly, the hash value of the content. The FileLib folder is essentially the store where the files themselves are held and referenced with the hash stored in the DataLib folder. We should be aware of the content library and understand the basics of how it works to aid our understanding of how best to troubleshoot. The following blog post from Microsoft does a good job of explaining the content library and its structure along with some information on its behavior: https://blogs.technet.microsoft.com/configmgrteam/2013/10/29/understanding-the-configuration-manager-content-library/.

The second application for the distribution point is SMS_DP_SMSSIG$ that resolves directly to the SMSSIG$ administrative share as opposed to a folder. This share, in turn, is stored in the folder by the same name on the drive we chose at install time. Inside this folder, we will find numerous .tar files that contain the signatures for the content.

A distribution point also uses a number of WMI classes in the ROOT\SCCMDP namespace. The classes in this namespace are listed as follows:

- SMS_DistributionPoint
- SMS_PackagesInContLib
- SMS_PullDPContentState
- SMS_PullDPNotification
- SMS_PullDPState
- SMS_SchemaVersion

In these classes, we can find information about the state of the distribution point and also the content held on the distribution point. We have already covered WMI in a previous chapter, so we can use the WMI tools from our troubleshooting toolkit in *Chapter 1, The Configuration Manager Troubleshooting Toolkit*, to work with, identify, and resolve any problematic behavior with a distribution point.

Pull distribution points

Pull distribution points are a feature that was first introduced into Configuration Manager in version 2012 SP1. The concept is really very simple. When we designate a distribution point as a pull distribution point, it has the ability to pull content from another distribution point instead of directly from the site server. We can specify numerous source distribution points so that the server can get content from more than one location, which can provide some great options when working with a large implementation where either sites are daisy-chained or certain network routes are preferred. An added bonus of this is that they perform better than a full distribution point when scaled, and this, as a result, gives us a theoretical increase in the number of distribution points available per site when combined with standard distribution points.

Something to remember when using pull distribution points is that when we distribute content to the server, the content must be first available on one of the source distribution points. This can often confuse administrators as they see status messages reporting that content has not been distributed to the distribution point when it is simply waiting for the source to update.

 Why not create a distribution point group for your source distribution point and your pull distribution point together. This way you should always have content reaching your pull distribution point.

A pull distribution point has one specific log file, `C:\Windows\CCM\Logs\PullDP.log`, which is stored on the server that holds the role.

This log file specifically records details of content transfers between the source and destination distribution point. If we suspect that there are problems with a pull distribution point, then this is one of the first places to go and check.

Cloud distribution points

Another feature first introduced in Configuration Manager 2012 SP1 was cloud distribution points. This is a variation on a standard distribution point and allows us to utilize our Microsoft Azure subscription to host a distribution point in the cloud. There are many advantages to this which are common with most cloud technologies that can be very useful, specifically in a large-scale distributed organization. We should be aware that although this role can be used as a fallback location for content, this is not a full distribution point and doesn't run a full server that we can make a remote desktop connection to, for example. Therefore, from a Configuration Manager point of view, there is a relatively limited amount of troubleshooting available when compared to a standard distribution point. We simply get an amount of storage available to us in Microsoft Azure and, as can be expected, particularly in a pay-as-you-go scenario, we can and would want to set some storage and transfer thresholds for alerting. These alerts will only appear in the Configuration Manager console in the **Monitoring** | **Overview** | **Alerts** workspace, so it is definitely worthwhile creating e-mail subscriptions for these. We will also be able to see this resource listed in our Microsoft Azure subscription and standard Azure-based troubleshooting applies from that regard.

It is also worth noting that cloud distribution points also have their own log files and do not necessarily appear in the same way as the standard log files. Both of these files are stored on the site system server by default in `%ProgramFiles%\Microsoft Configuration Manager\Logs\`:

* `CloudMgr.log`
* `CloudDP-<guid>.log`

The former contains general information about cloud distribution points in general from a Configuration Manager perspective. If there are one or more cloud distribution points, this file will contain information about all the storage and bandwidth statistics as well as recording information about the provisioning of content and any Configuration Manager administrator actions to change the state of the service that runs a cloud distribution point. The latter log file contains more specific information about a cloud distribution point and is named according to the GUID associated with that distribution point. This file contains details about storage and content access for that distribution point only.

Preboot Execution Environment

The distribution point role offers the choice of enabling PXE to act as the network boot host for client machines. This is commonly used in OSD scenarios and is generally utilized quite heavily by many organizations. Just for the record, in versions of Configuration Manager prior to version 2012, this was a separate role. PXE services in Configuration Manager are based on **Windows Deployment Services (WDS)**. WDS will be automatically installed as part of the distribution point role installation if this option is selected and it isn't already installed. Although WDS is utilized, Configuration Manager uses it purely as a platform and implements its own customization by adding a folder structure and custom boot images instead of using the default WDS files. The `RemoteInstall` folder is used in the same way as WDS, but we will find the following three extra folders over a standard WDS install:

- `SMSBoot`
- `SMSImages`
- `SMSTemp`

Without going into too much detail, the `SMSBoot` folder contains the files required to actually perform the network boot. The `SMSImages` folder contains the boot images that we distribute to the distribution point from the Configuration Manager console. Finally, the `SMSTemp` folder is simply a temporary location used when boot images are updated.

There are several ports required for PXE booting and OSD that should be open where necessary on the distribution point server firewall and on any other firewalls between the client and the server:

- `UDP 67`: For Dynamic Host Configuration Protocol (DHCP)
- `UDP 68`: For Dynamic Host Configuration Protocol (DHCP)
- `UDP 69`: For Trivial File Transfer Protocol (TFTP)
- `UDP 4011`: Boot Information Negotiation Layer (BINL)

Something else to consider when using PXE are any DHCP options that we may require on the DHCP server. In theory, we need not configure anything on your DHCP server; however, in practice, it is often the case in many environments where the relevant options need to be specified either by necessity or choice. This can be for a number of reasons including security policies or if multiple network boot providers are available on the network. The following ports may sometimes be required:

- `Option 66`: TFTP server name
- `Option 67`: Boot file name

There is also a third option that should be used if the DHCP server is also the PXE server:

- `Option 60`: Client Identifier

It is also worth noting that it can sometimes be useful to configure IP Helpers on the gateway of a subnet that can allow these services to traverse multiple subnets. By default, the network boot capabilities will only be available to the network it resides on. This is worth considering when troubleshooting issues including network boots responding from unexpected locations; however, this can also be a boundary-related issue.

Finally, we should understand the basic process of the handshake that takes place between a client and a distribution point when performing a network boot of a machine with Configuration Manager PXE. This will assist in troubleshooting PXE boot problems with Configuration Manager and, at least, identify at which point in the process the problem occurs. PXE boot problems are fairly common with Configuration Manager; however, majority of the time this is down due to environmental issues such as networking or user error such as incorrect hardware addresses. At a high level, the following is the order in which the PXE boot works:

1. **DHCP Discovery** — client broadcasts looking for an IP address from DHCP and a PXE service.
2. **Configuration Manager Check** — Configuration Manager as the PXE provider looks up the device.
3. **DHCP Offer** — once Configuration Manager has checked, there is something for the device to run there is a DHCP offer with IP and PXE provider.
4. **DHCP Request** — client makes the DHCP request for IP as a broadcast.
5. **DHCP Acknowledgement** — DHCP server acknowledges the IP lease as a broadcast.
6. **DHCP Request** — client now unicasts for the PXE boot server and boot file.
7. **DHCP Acknowledgement** — PXE server acknowledges the request and the bootstrap file starts to download.
8. **DHCP Request** — client makes another unicast request for PXE with architecture included.
9. **Configuration Manager Check** — Configuration Manager as the PXE provider checks that there is a PXE enabled deployment for the device.
10. **DHCP Acknowledgement** — PXE server acknowledges the request with the boot server and boot file.
11. **Download starts** — the download of the boot file and WinPE now begins.

Troubleshooting our distribution point

Now that we have an understanding of the various features and functions of a distribution point, we should get down to the different ways in which we can troubleshoot it and what resources we have available to do so.

Console

As always, the console will provide us with good high-level, at-a-glance information about the health state of our distribution points. Looking first in the **Monitoring | Overview | Distribution Status** workspace, we will see that we can take a look at the following items:

- Content Status
- Distribution Point Group Status
- Distribution Point Configuration Status

Content Status

The Content Status workspace will show us various details of each content item including its distribution status, which can be viewed in the lower half of the split pane view. We should note that the pie chart shown in the following screenshot is relative to the number of distribution points that the content has been distributed to:

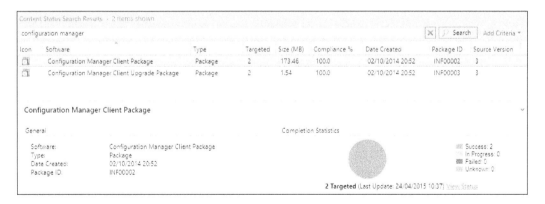

From this view, we can click on the **View Status** link to take us to a more detailed view of the content item. Here we can see which distribution points the content distributed to successfully or otherwise. This is particularly useful to get a quick glance as an indicator if we have a troublesome content item that has issues being distributed.

Distribution Point Group Status

This workspace will cover all distribution point groups in our site and similar to the content status will give us a high-level red, amber, green status of our distribution point group. Selecting **View Status** will again take us to a more detailed view in the same template as content status but relevant to the distribution points within that group. This is particularly useful to get a quick glance as an indicator if we have a troublesome distribution point within a group.

Distribution Point Configuration Status

The configuration status view is another at-a-glance view—this time for the configuration state of our distribution point. This includes whether PXE, multicast, or content validation is enabled on our distribution point complete with a message count for that server and a success, in progress, warning, or error status icon. The status icons are only governed by the validation of content on the distribution point and not by any configuration options.

The status rules are as follows and all content is classed as a package when it comes to distribution:

Rule	Status Code	Status
If the package count on the DP equals the number of packages that the Configuration Manager database thinks should be installed.	1	Success
If the package count on the DP equals the number of packages that the Configuration Manager database thinks should be installed and there are packages in progress.	2	In Progress
If the package count on the DP equals the number of packages that the Configuration Manager database thinks should be installed, there are packages in progress, and there are also some package errors.	4	Warning
Any other condition	5	Error

Each time a package is distributed, the content is validated and a comparison made between the site copy and the distribution point copy. This is how the package count is made and used in a comparison to produce the resultant status. The status messages available in this view are also very useful as they give us a slightly lower level of detail regarding the processing activity and configuration changes for the distribution point.

Logs

We have covered log files in general in an earlier chapter, but as distribution points have a fundamental role in Configuration Manager, we should also be aware of a the specific log files which apply. Unless stated otherwise, these log files can be found in the `\\<DPServer>\SMS_DP$\sms\logs`.

LogFile	Description
`smsdpprov.log`	This file will give us all the information about extraction of the files on the distribution point that are compressed when stored. This file is found on the distribution point itself unless it is on the same server as the site server.
`smsdpusage.log`	This log file contains information about the `smsdpusage.exe` process, which is scheduled to run each day on distribution points and records distribution point summary usage based on IIS logs.

LogFile	Description
`smspxe.log`	As we might expect from the name, this file holds details about PXE responses provided by the site system to clients and also includes information about the expansion of the boot images and boot files in the `RemoteInstall` folder.
`pulldp_install. log`	If we have enabled the distribution point as a pull distribution point, then this is the installation log which will show us the return code with verbose logging of the installation.
`smsdpmon.log`	This log file relates to the `smsdpmon.exe` process. That process is the content validation process and will only run if we enable it on the distribution point. The log file contains success and failure messages for validation.

WMI

On a distribution point, there is a WMI database that holds account of all the content that was distributed to it. This is stored in the WMI namespace ROOT\SCCMDP and the class we should look at is SMS_PackagesInContLib.

We could use the following PowerShell on a distribution point to check for the existence of an item on a distribution point as sometimes we can experience mismatches between the site server and the distribution point. This will then validate whether the distribution point itself has a record of the package as the view in the console will reflect what the site database thinks we have on the distribution point.

```
Get-WmiObject -Namespace root\sccmdp -Class SMS_PackagesInContLib |
Where-Object PackageID -eq 'INF00005'
```

If a package is found, the output will be similar to the following:

```
__GENUS            : 2
__CLASS            : SMS_PackagesInContLib
__SUPERCLASS       :
__DYNASTY          : SMS_PackagesInContLib
__RELPATH          : SMS_PackagesInContLib.PackageID="INF00005"
__PROPERTY_COUNT   : 2
__DERIVATION       : {}
__SERVER           : DEMO-DPM01
```

```
__NAMESPACE          : ROOT\sccmdp
__PATH               : \\DEMO-DPM01\ROOT\sccmdp:SMS_PackagesInContLib.
PackageID="INF00005"
PackageID            : INF00005
PackageShareLocation :
PSComputerName       : DEMO-DPM01
```

We should obviously replace the `PackageID` with the value we are looking for. This task can also be carried out using any of the WMI tools listed in the troubleshooting toolkit. However, PowerShell is flexible in that we can swap the value for a variable and even make a quick script to prompt each time.

On occasion, we can also see errors like the following reported in the console and in the `smsdpmon.log`:

```
"The package data in WMI is not consistent to PkgLib"
```

or

```
"Package INF00005 can't be found in PkgLib"
```

These are typical of content mismatches. After making some checks in the console and with the preceding PowerShell, we can add a | `Remove-WmiObject` to the PowerShell to remove the content if it is orphaned.

PXE

Troubleshooting PXE can be somewhat of a minefield and is often dependent on environmental factors such as DHCP options and networking. In conjunction with the process explained earlier in this chapter, it is suggested that we bookmark one of the lists that are available through a web search as they give reasonable explanation of the problems associated with PXE errors. Some of the common error codes experienced with Configuration Manager are among this list and are given as follows:

Code	Description	Typical Symptom
PXE-E51	No DHCP or proxy DHCP offers were received.	The client cannot contact the DHCP or PXE server, check network connectivity, firewalls, and routing, particularly if across subnets.
PXE-E53	No boot filename was received.	The DHCP option 67 is specified and it should not be, or is specified incorrectly.

Code	Description	Typical Symptom
N/A	TFTP download failed.	This can occur once the TFTP download has started. As previously, check DHCP options and ensure an x86 and x64 boot image are distributed to the server.
PXE-E61	Media test failed, check cable.	Speaks for itself really, make cable and network connection checks.
PXE-E3B	TFTP error: File not found.	This generally means that the SMSBoot folder is empty, and you should redistribute x86 and x64 images.
PXE-E55	Proxy DHCP service did not reply to request on port 4011.	Check that your DHCP options are specified correctly and that the relevant services are running on those servers.
PXE-T01	The specified file was not found Or File not found	The PXE server is responding to the request; however, the file that it instructs the client to boot to is not there. A redistribution or validation of the boot image may resolve this.
PXE-T04	Access violation.	This can occur in combination with the next two error codes. Commonly it can refer to the DHCP options being incorrectly configured.
PXE-E36	Error Received from TFTP Server.	As in the previous message, this most commonly suggests that the boot file (DHCP option 67) is incorrectly specified.
PXE-M0F	Exiting PXE Rom.	This is simply a notification that the client is exiting the PXE process and is commonly seen in combination with other errors at the end of an error list.
PXE-E78	Could not locate boot server.	Similar to PXE-E36 but this refers to the boot server name, which is specified where applicable in DHCP option 66.

This is by no means an exhaustive list; therefore, it is suggested we reference a web search for a specific error outside of this. We should also not rule out a very common factor, however, which is normally between the desk and the chair. It is a very common problem that a mistyped MAC address was entered during the import of a manual machine entry record, and, in many cases, this is the most common PXE-related issue seen.

Distribution point common issues

There can be various problems seen with distribution points but there are some issues that seem to be more frequent than others. Let us take a look at the common issues that can occur with a distribution point.

Distribution

Really simple, the content has not been distributed to the distribution point. This might be the person clicking on the buttons, it might be mismatched content, or it might be the result of a delayed distribution due to a pull distribution point or network delays. Whichever way, we shouldn't discount checking the basics as a quick rule-in or rule-out exercise.

Boundary assignment

Boundaries define where a client can obtain content from; if they are not correct, then it simply will not work. Often in large or distributed organizations, IP subnets can change without notification, which can leave a Configuration Manager scratching their head. There is little worse than troubleshooting the unknown; therefore, it is worth implementing a process with our networking administrators to ensure we are informed when such information changes. We should also validate that our boundaries are correct in the first instance as we don't want to be pulling content over the wide area network without good reason as this can often explain slow content download.

Content mismatch

Whenever a new Configuration Manager installation is implemented, it is recommended we ensure that content validation is enabled on each distribution point. Content mismatches were quite common in previous versions of Configuration Manager and are now less common; however, they still do appear from time to time in current versions of the product. This is most notably highlighted in the Distribution Point Configuration Status in the console. This can be found in **Monitoring | Overview | Distribution Status | Distribution Point Configuration Status**.

Often, a quick resolution to this is to simply redistribute the content to the distribution point that will validate it once the distribution is complete. For more detailed troubleshooting on this, you can refer to this blog post:

```
http://wmug.co.uk/wmug/b/peter_egerton/archive/2014/03/19/
configuration-manager-dp-configuration-status-and-content-validation
```

BranchCache

We have not discussed BranchCache before now as the technology is not specific to Configuration Manager. That said, Configuration Manager has options to use this for peer-to-peer sharing of content across subnets. This sounds great in theory; however, in practice, it is not always 100 percent successful and can be affected by delays or cleared caches. Troubleshooting BranchCache is not straightforward either and involves checking often cryptic event logs in Microsoft-Windows-BranchCache / Operational to decipher if it is working. There are, however, some BranchCache usage reports available from a great company called **2Pint Software** that provides them for free. These can be very useful when troubleshooting any BranchCache transfers, specifically in a Configuration Manager environment: http://2pintsoftware.com/products/branchcache-reporting/.

Prestaged content

Something that can sometimes catch administrators out is prestaged content on a distribution point. Similar to the initial point about distribution, we should remember that if we distribute to a distribution point that is marked for prestaged content, then the content may not be delivered if we have not configured the content accordingly.

PXE boot failure

OSD is a major feature in Configuration Manager and PXE booting is probably the most common method for building machines. As we discussed already, there are a number of factors that can influence the outcome of a successful PXE deployment. Probably, the most common factor in PXE issues is the supporting IT infrastructure. Once we have it installed and working, then it generally will remain as such until something changes.

Summary

Throughout this chapter, we have looked at the fundamental roles of Configuration Manager as the management point and the distribution point. We have looked at the workings of each role, which is beneficial to understand. This remains the most valuable fragment of information when troubleshooting. To think of the functionality provided by these roles, it can be surprising how simple the architecture really is. The HTTP codes that we discussed for the management points are transferable to other roles; however, they are probably most prominent on this role in particular. This is definitely information to remember for multiple troubleshooting purposes. We have also looked at common problems with both roles that are based both on personal experience and issues discussed within the Configuration Manager community across user groups and forums. As usual, there are a number of ways to troubleshoot these issues with various tools, and it is simply a matter of choosing the correct one, finding a starting point, and then applying the logic based on our knowledge of how the role works.

In the next chapter, we will cover other roles available in Configuration Manager and discuss the common issues and what to check. We will also look at what the impact can be of the rest of Configuration Manager if that role is not functioning. Often it is worthwhile understanding both the impact of a nonfunctioning role and the wider impact in a *cut your losses* scenario where we may decide to remove the role completely.

6
Troubleshooting Other Roles

Now that we have looked at the two most common roles in Configuration Manager, we also need to know how to tackle the rest of the roles. Most installations of Configuration Manager are very likely to have at least some of these roles, but perhaps not all of them. However, it is beneficial to understand something about each role. We will take a look at how each of these roles can affect the rest of our Configuration Manager environment when they are in a state of disorder, and then how we go about troubleshooting them. We will also look at roles from Configuration Manager current branch and see what troubleshooting options are available for these. We will look at the out of band service point and Windows Intune connector, which were in 2012 versions of Configuration Manager but are deprecated for current branch, which is also known as version 1511. Where multiple roles are associated with each other we will look at them in conjunction to help ease understanding of their functions and how to troubleshoot them.

The roles that we will be looking at in this chapter are as follows:

- Application catalog roles
- Asset intelligence synchronization point
- Certificate registration point
- Endpoint protection point
- Enrollment and enrollment proxy point
- Fallback status point
- Out of band service point
- Reporting services point
- Service connection point
- Software update point
- State migration point
- System health validator point
- Windows Intune connector

Application Catalog roles

Here we will cover both the Application Catalog website point and the Application Catalog web service point, as these roles are used together to provide the functionality of the Application Catalog to our end users. For clarification, this is the self-service web portal that our users can connect to in order to install the applications that we have made available to them. This should not be confused with the Software Center, which is available by default on all Configuration Manager client machines and allows installation of software that was made available to our device.

Application Catalog website point

Like many roles in Configuration Manager, this site role is a web application that is hosted on **Internet Information Services (IIS)** and therefore many of the same troubleshooting approaches used with any web application will apply. We can use the standard HTTP error code list from our troubleshooting toolkit in *Chapter 1, The Configuration Manager Troubleshooting Toolkit*, to give us an idea of where the problem lies. This role is unlike a management point or distribution point in terms of structure, because when we browse the web application we will see that there are elements that will be more similar to a typical web application complete with a `web.config` file and cascading style sheets. We should not make any changes to this structure or content directly; however, we should be aware of it and its location, which by default is `%ProgramFiles%\SMS_CCM\CMApplicationCatalog`.

Troubleshooting in the console

With regard to the Configuration Manager console, this role is one of the less visible components, and troubleshooting from here is minimal. From the Monitoring workspace, we can browse to **System Status | Site Status** and get a quick indicator on the status of the Application Catalog website point. This status is based on a cumulative count of status messages for the component `SMS_PORTALWEB_CONTROL_MANAGER` and refreshes by default every day at 00:00, so bear this in mind when using this as it is only a point in time indication and may not truly represent the current status. Incidentally, we can change this interval using the Status Summarizers window in the site properties. Also be aware that if we right-click or use the ribbon to show messages, then the status message viewer displays relevant messages for the site system itself and not necessarily the individual component. Moving on from here, we can specifically view the component's status by browsing to the **System Status | Component Status** view and selecting or filtering on `SMS_PORTALWEB_CONTROL_MANAGER`. This will again give us an indication of status, either **OK**, **Warning**, or **Failed**. If we go to the properties of this component in the same view, then we can observe the thresholds defined for each status. These, by default, are as follows:

	Warning	**Critical**
Error messages	1	5
Warning messages	10	50
Informational messages	2000	5000

We can, of course, change these threshold levels in the **Component Status Summarizer** properties, which can be found in **Administration | Site Configuration | Sites**. As with all views in the **Monitoring** workspace where there are aggregated status indicators, be sure that the counters are reset if changes have been made to resolve problems, otherwise the status indicators may not turn green until up to 24 hours later.

Moving on a little further, we can show specific messages for the SMS_PORTALWEB_ CONTROL_MANAGER component using either the ribbon or right-click menu. This, of course, gives us a greater level of detail than the monitoring indicators but not as much as the log files that are provided. As this particular role is quite static in terms of frequency of configuration change, the common status messages in this view generally give information about component availability. The Status Message Viewer will also display information regarding the success of your role's installation. A common mistake for this particular role seems to be not fully installing and configuring the prerequisites, specifically around IIS and ASP.NET 4.0. Let us not forget, however, that this particular role is in fact a tangible role that can be seen and touched by the end user, and so, inevitably, this can mean that any problems with this role are automatically highlighted to you through the helpdesk.

Troubleshooting in the log files

There are three log files dedicated to this site system role, two for the initial installation or setup and one for the ongoing running of the component. The SMSPORTALWEBSetup.log and portlwebMSI.log files are found by default in %ProgramFiles%\Microsoft Configuration Manager\Logs and contain information about the installation and uninstallation of the Application Catalog website point site system role. Don't forget that even if the installation wizard shows as completed and the role is added to the console, we should really check the SMSPORTALWEBSetup.log file to ensure that we have a successful installation. This is signified by these three lines at the end of the log file:

```
portlweb.msi exited with return code: 0

Installation was successful.

~RoleSetup().
```

If we see anything other than a return code 0 for the `portlweb.msi` then we should make note of the return code and use the Windows Installer Errors Reference mentioned in *Chapter 1*, *The Configuration Manager Troubleshooting Toolkit*. We can also look at the more detailed `portlwebMSI.log` file and see exactly what went wrong. Generally, we can look for the return code we noted and then work back from that point to see what may have caused the failure to install or uninstall.

Once we have achieved a successful installation we can use the `ServicePortalWebsite.log` file found by default in `%ProgramFiles%\SMS_CCM\CMApplicationCatalog` to investigate the cause of any issues with the Application Catalog website point. Typically, this log file would contain information about website starts and stops along with heartbeat checks and any HTTP responses in the case of a failure. A normally functioning role would typically repeat something like this in the `ServicePortalWebsite.log` file every hour:

```
SoftwareCatalog website - application instance dispose ...

No cached apps to serialize (caching not enabled or no apps in cache)

SoftwareCatalog website stop ...

SoftwareCatalog website - application instance dispose ...

SoftwareCatalog website start ...

DefaultApplicationOfferService - retrieving client proxy using endpoint
SecureBinding_IApplicationOfferService

FindCertificate - Found certs via FindByThumbprint, count = 1

DefaultApplicationOfferService - opening channel via client proxy

DefaultApplicationOfferService - opened service session
urn:uuid:109b8ac0-5962-41b3-b376-fbe1317cc9d1

ServiceProxy - BeginCheckServiceHeartbeat

ServiceProxy - BeginCheckServiceHeartbeat done

AppCacheableBase - configured writable app directory set to: C:\Program
Files\SMS_CCM\CMApplicationCatalog\Content\Images\AppIcons

ASP.NET application cache will NOT be used (either cache dir not found,
asp.net cache is not set, or cache setting in web.config is <= 0

ServiceProxy - EndCheckServiceHeartbeat done

Warmup complete

No language specified in Request.UserLanguages

SoftwareCatalog website - requested resource: ~/default.aspx, api-
version: ""

No current build version found so will try to get one

Got 5.0.8239.1000 build version
```

Any configuration issues with the role will be reported in this log file and should be investigated and remediated accordingly, but generally speaking this tends to be a trouble-free role. We can check role configuration in the registry by looking at the `Computer\HKEY_LOCAL_MACHINE\SOFTWARE\Microsoft\SMS\PORTALWEB\` key.

This can often be worth a check for incorrect information in the case of a configuration-related error because, along with a lot of other roles, the site database will expect one configuration and the site system server will also have a configuration, which in this case is stored in the registry. Sometimes there can be a mismatch between the database and the site system server, particularly if there have been multiple installations and uninstallations. We can also reference the logging subkey and extend the log file size and history if required. This also applies to the web service point, and we will look at how to do this in the next section.

Application Catalog web service point

Similar to the Application Catalog website point, there is actually a limited amount of configuration needed for the installation of the server role. This is reflected by the troubleshooting of this role and you may be happy to learn that there are many similarities with the Application Catalog website point when trying to fix any problem.

Troubleshooting in the console

If we take a look at the role configuration in **Administration | Site Configuration | Servers and Site System Roles**, we can see that there is actually very little in terms of configuration that we can actually change. We just see the web application name, its website, and the port numbers. In fact, we can't actually change anything, so with that in mind we can be reasonably confident that if the role previously worked and it is not working now, then the issue is very likely to be elsewhere.

Troubleshooting in the log files

If this is the first installation of the role and it therefore has not worked previously, then we can check to ensure that the installation has completed using the following log files, which can be found by default in `%ProgramFiles%\Microsoft Configuration Manager\Logs`:

- `SMSAWEBSVCSetup.log`
- `awebsvcMSI.log`

The MSI log, which details the output from the Microsoft Installer, is the more detailed of the two. The setup log shows a slightly more summarized output from the installation process. Remember that when we run through the installation from the Configuration Manager console and we get a green tick, it does not necessarily indicate that the role is installed; it merely shows that the role has been added to the console and the installation has been started. We are essentially looking for the last three lines of the setup log file to read as follows:

```
awebsvc.msi exited with return code: 0

Installation was successful.

~RoleSetup().
```

This represents a successful installation. If we have something different, then check the return code and work from there. A common issue with the installation of this role seems to be when the last three lines show an exit code of 123:

```
WCF is not activated

Installation Failed. Error Code: 123

~RoleSetup().
```

As the error suggests, one of the prerequisite features, which is **Windows Communication Foundation (WCF)**, has not been installed or activated. In this case, we should check this in our server roles and features and ensure we have all the necessary prerequisites for our operating system version. Be aware that these can be slightly different for pre and post Windows Server 2012.

> A role installation will retry every 60 minutes, or we can simply uninstall, wait, and then reinstall the role if we prefer.
> A further option, which applies to all roles, is to restart the SMS_SITE_COMPONENT_MANAGER service on the site server, which will initiate a retry on the component installation that failed.

As this role is again a web application, we can use the same troubleshooting methods that apply to any standard IIS application and any error codes can be referenced from the HTTP status code lists we talked about in *Chapter 1*, *The Configuration Manager Troubleshooting Toolkit*. There are, however, some specific log files for this server role, which can found in the logs folder of the application, which is stored by default on the server where the role is installed, in the %ProgramFiles%\SMS_CCM\CMApplicationCatalogSvc folder.

Inside the logs folder there is the `ServicePortalWebService.log` file which contains some information about the `ApplicationOfferService` and the `DeviceManagementService`, which are the two components of this web application. This log file can be extended in size and the amount of history stored by changing the default decimal values in the registry from 8 MB (8000000 bytes) and one history file. The registry key we need is at `Computer\HKEY_LOCAL_MACHINE\SOFTWARE\Microsoft\SMS\AWEBSVC\Logging`.

Let's take a look at the following screenshot:

Name	Type	Data
(Default)	REG_SZ	(value not set)
AdminUILog	REG_SZ	C:\Program Files\SMS_CCM\CMApplicationCatalogSvc\Logs\
LogMaxHistory	REG_DWORD	0x00000001 (1)
MaxFileSize	REG_DWORD	0x007a1200 (8000000)

Generally speaking, this role is not usually prone to frequent errors, so we should deal with each one as it comes. As with anything, the more frequently we change the component and its configuration, the greater the chance of something going wrong.

Asset Intelligence synchronization point

The Asset Intelligence synchronization point is a component that rarely arises as a problematic role. The footprint is really quite light, and indeed in a worst case scenario it is no great chore to actually uninstall and reinstall. That said, however, we should know what makes up the Asset Intelligence synchronization point in order to be able to perform some basic troubleshooting before we get to the uninstall stage. The components that make up the component are minimal; we will find a folder located on the relevant server by default in `%Program Files%\AIUS`. Within that folder we will find just two files:

* `AIUpdateSVC.exe`
* `AIUpdateSVC.exe.config`

The `.exe` file is the actual service that represents the synchronization point, and the `.config` file is, of course, the configuration file for the service. This service is also represented as a Windows service named `AI_UPDATE_SERVICE_POINT`, which can be stopped and restarted at will from the Configuration Manager Service Manager should we experience any problems.

Troubleshooting in the console

We can, of course, check the status of the role from within the **Monitoring** workspace of the console by browsing to **System Status | Component Status** and looking for the `AI_UPDATE_SERVICE_POINT` component. As usual, from here we can right-click and show relevant messages for this component and also go to the properties to view the thresholds for warning and critical states. In reality, that is really about as much as we can check from the console for this site role. We should, nonetheless, also be aware that as this role requires Internet access, the site that hosts this role should have the correct proxy server specified if applicable. In **Administration | Site Configuration | Servers and Site System Roles**, look at the properties of the site system role and check the proxy server is correct along with the port. Whilst here, it is also worth checking that the account credentials used for this are still correct and valid; however, should this be the case, it is highly likely that we would notice problems on any other site roles that rely on an Internet connection, such as a software update point or Microsoft Intune Connector.

Troubleshooting in the log files

There are three log files specifically associated with the Asset Intelligence synchronization point and they can all be found by default in `%ProgramFiles%\ Microsoft Configuration Manager\Logs` folder. The logs are as follows:

- `AIUSSetup.log`
- `AIUSMSI.log`
- `AIUpdateSvc.log`

As the name suggests, `AIUSSetup.log` refers to the installation of the role and is relatively short but contains information about the tasks performed and the success or failure of the installation. As always, we are looking for an `Installation was successful` message on the penultimate line.

The log file, `AIUSMSI.log`, goes into quite a lot more detail about the steps taken to install the site role and service. If we suspect the role didn't install correctly for some reason, then this log file will give us the most useful information about where this may have failed, so open it with CMTrace and look out for the highlighted lines. We are always looking for a `MainEngineThread is returning 0` message on the penultimate line of the log file to signify a successful install.

Assuming that the role has installed successfully, we only have a single log file to pay attention to, `AIUpdateSvc.log`, which does make things somewhat easier than troubleshooting some other roles. The default logging level for this role is informational only, which is normally sufficient, but if we find that this doesn't give us the information we are looking for, we can change the logging level to one of the following levels:

- All
- Verbose
- Information
- Warning
- Critical
- Error
- ActivityTracing
- Off

To do this, we need to edit the `AIUpdateSVC.exe.config` file as an administrator and look for the `<switches>` tag, like so:

```
<switches>
        <!--Value can be the members of the SourceLevel enum. These are
"All", "Verbose", "Information",
             Warning", "Critical", "Error", "Off", "ActivityTracing"
        -->
        <add name="sourceSwitch" value="Information" />
    </switches>
```

In the `<add name="sourceSwitch"` line, we can amend the value to be that of one in the aforementioned list. It should be noted that logging levels do include all information from a lower level, that is, a warning level includes everything from information and then more besides. Once we have changed and saved the file we will need to restart the `AI_UPDATE_SERVICE_POINT` service and the desired logging level will be applied. This change will be reflected in the log file, as shown below:

```
Asset Intelligence Catalog Sync Service Information: 0 :
Asset Intelligence Catalog Sync Service Verbose: 0 :
```

Information is the default logging level and is normally sufficient for most circumstances but the options are there if we require them.

Certificate registration point

This role gives us the ability to provision client certification to managed devices, such as an Apple Mac, and mobile devices using Configuration Manager. This component is quite a specific role and would not usually be implemented in a typical Configuration Manager deployment. That said, certain organizations may well have a specific requirement for this to be installed, so in that case we should know how to work with the role and maintain functionality in case of a problem.

This Configuration Manager role acts as a go-between for a device such as an Apple Mac or mobile device to communicate with a **Network Device Enrollment Service** (**NDES**) in order to utilize the widely used **Simple Certificate Enrollment Protocol** (**SCEP**). The acronym for this should not be confused with the endpoint protection feature of Configuration Manager as they are very different things. The certificate registration point is another web application that runs from IIS and, as always, the standard IIS troubleshooting methods should apply alongside the role-specific troubleshooting resources.

Troubleshooting in the console

From the console we can use the component status view in **Overview | System Status | Component Status** and look for the SMS_CERTIFICATE_REGISTRATION_POINT component. This gives us a quick indication of the status of the component based on a count of status messages since 00:00:00 by default. As there are a number of prerequisites required for the certificate registration point, it is always beneficial to check the status messages after an installation of this role as the installation wizard simply confirms that the installation has been initiated. If we have a prerequisite missing, such as an invalid or missing certificate on the server, then this will not be reported in the wizard but will show up in the status messages. The prerequisites list can be found on the Microsoft TechNet library (https://technet.microsoft.com/en-us/library/gg682077.aspx?#BKMK_SiteSystemRolePrereqs).

A failed installation is signified by an ID 1016 message and a missing or invalid certificate is signified by an ID 4964 message. Missing or misconfigured prerequisites are a common reason for the failure of this installation as there are a number of things to install and configure, including IIS, NDES, the Configuration Manager Policy Module, and a CA with appropriate certificates. With this in mind, it is advisable to validate each of these prerequisites individually prior to installation and also in the case of any issue, as there are many moving parts and any one could prevent the role from functioning correctly. We are not going to go into the details of each component individually in this book as they all have their own features and prerequisites, but it suffices to say there are a number of web pages out there with sufficient information to get us started.

Troubleshooting in the log files

There are a number of log files dedicated to this role; two are relevant to the installation only, and the rest contain information about the ongoing running of the role.

In the default `%ProgramFiles%\Microsoft Configuration Manager\Logs` folder we have:

- `CRPSetup.log`
- `CRPMSI.log`
- `CRPCtrl.log`
- `NDESPlugin.log`

In the default `%ProgramFiles%\SMS_CCM\CRP\Logs` folder we have – `CRP.log`.

The log file, `CRPSetup.log`, contains setup information at a fairly high level and, as usual, look out for the return code at the end of the log file which should always return `0`. If the installation failed, we will see this on the penultimate line:

Fatal MSI Error - CRP.msi could not be installed

In this case, we should refer to the `CRPMSI.log` file, which contains more detailed information, giving a line by line output of the installation activities, including where any failures may be. As this log file is quite verbose, it is recommended that we use CMTrace to read this log file. The most obvious lines are highlighted as they will contain such words as error or fail, which makes the whole troubleshooting process much simpler.

The log file, `CRPCtrl.log`, shows us the health of the component by logging routine checks against the component's availability and is a good place to check for occasions when the whole component is suspected to be nonfunctional. This log file checks for the availability of the correct certificates and appropriate permissions to them, along with validating certificate thumbprints, and runs by default every 10 minutes. If we would like to force a health check, then we can restart the `SMS_CERTIFICATE_REGISTRATION_POINT` service on the server that hosts the role.

The log file, `NDESPlugin.log`, goes a little outside of the boundaries of Configuration Manager, as this role requires a specific Configuration Manager plugin from the installation media, which is applied to the NDES server. This is the log file that records challenge verification activities. If there are problems experienced with certificate enrollment, then this would be one of the first places to check.

Finally, the `CRP.log file` records the actual enrollment activities on the Certificate Enrollment point. Again, if there are certificate enrollment issues, then this would be one of the first places to check for errors.

As we know, this role is based on IIS and is also secured with a certificate as it is a HTTPS role. We can browse to the address of the component (`https://<CRP_FQDN>/CMCertificateRegistration`) and, if configured correctly, should receive a **403 Forbidden** response, which is okay.

If we see any other response, then the role and its prerequisites are not fully or correctly configured. If this is the case, then we can start to use the log files to look further into the problem. We can also increase the amount of logging performed on this role by amending the number of log files and also the size of each log file. This can be done by browsing the registry and adjusting the `LogMaxHistory` and `MaxFileSize` values in the `Computer\HKEY_LOCAL_MACHINE\SOFTWARE\Microsoft\SMS\CRP\Logging` registry key.

Endpoint Protection point

As the name suggests, the Endpoint Protection point deals with the System Center Endpoint Protection functionality of the product. This functionality was introduced with System Center 2012 Configuration Manager and incorporates the now defunct Microsoft Forefront Protection 2010. This feature provides us with endpoint protection for our Configuration Manager in the form of antimalware and firewalling using the Windows firewall. On first glance at the configuration of the role in the console, some people may be a little disappointed as the only options you have available are the Endpoint Protection License terms and the Microsoft Active Protection Service membership. There are, however, a few other places we can look to start troubleshooting this role, first of course being the **Monitoring** workspace of the console.

Troubleshooting in the console

The **Endpoint Protection Status** and **Malware Detected** views in the **Monitoring** workspace will only give us information about the status of the clients using Endpoint Protection and not the component itself. Still, it is useful information about the status of Endpoint Protection on our clients. We have a traffic light view of the success or failures of scanning or remediating clients and we are also given figures for the number of at-risk clients and malware detections. This can still be useful information in the troubleshooting of the component itself, though. If we take a point in time check and then revisit it sometime later, we can use that reference point to see if there is any improvement in success rates or increase in at-risk clients, for example. It all depends on what our specific issue is and what is raising our suspicion that we may have a problematic Endpoint Protection point. Also, don't forget to double-check the Endpoint Protection policies in the **Assets and Compliance workspace** under the `Endpoint Protection` folder. We can check the order of policy deployments are as expected and also add columns to the view to show the last modified date and the user that made the modifications in case a change has been made which has had a detrimental effect on Endpoint Protection. With the high-level checks covered, we can start to look a little closer by checking the `SMS_ENDPOINT_PROTECTION_MANAGER` and the `SMS_ENDPOINT_PROTECTION_CONTROL_MANAGER` components in the **Monitoring** workspace under **Overview | System Status | Component Status**. This again gives us an indication of the components that make up the Endpoint Protection point and shows the availability status. It is suggested that we add some extra columns to the view to show **Errors**, **Warnings**, **Last Heartbeat** and **Last Status Message**. We should also consider the **Heartbeat Interval** when reviewing this information. These things combined will give us a good indication of whether or not the role is functioning and reporting statuses to the site server.

Of course, from this point we can start to delve a little deeper into the status messages and the log files. From the component status view, which we should now be familiar with, we can right-click and show messages for all messages, errors, warnings or just information messages. It would normally be recommended to view all messages once we are familiar with reading the status messages, as this way we get the entire picture of what is going on in the site. It allows us to read through what the component has been doing at a halfway level between console and logs, which for many circumstances is sufficient information to resolve an issue without getting lost in the detail of the logs.

Troubleshooting in the log files

There are four log files in total that are specifically for System Center Endpoint Protection. Three of these files are located on the site server by default in the `%ProgramFiles%\Microsoft Configuration Manager\Logs` folder:

- `EPSetup.log`
- `EPMgr.log`
- `EPCtrlMgr.log`

There is also one other log file, which is stored on the client itself, and by default is in the `%WINDIR%\CCM\Logs` folder — `EndpointProtectionAgent.log`.

Going through these in order, the `EPSetup.log` file is where we can check for the installation status of the role. The log file isn't especially detailed, but we can use this as a quick check by locating the `Installation was successful` message on the penultimate line of the log file. Once the role has been installed on the server and the client, we can use `EPMgr.log` to keep check on the running of the site system role. This log file only really gives us information about the status of the component, whether that be up or down, and we would normally see simple detection alert check messages in the log file. The `EPCtrlMgr.log` file also gives us information regarding the synchronization of information about malware threats from the server that hosts the Endpoint Protection point role and the Configuration Manager database.

If we switch to the client itself, then we can use `EndpointProtectionAgent.log` to check the installation of Endpoint Protection and also how policies and new Endpoint Protection agent versions are applied to the client. This file should be used initially if we suspect that there are failures in either of these and we can use some of the information in the next section on policies to drill further into this.

Antimalware policies

When troubleshooting Endpoint Protection, a common problem can be the application of policies to a client. The first and easiest check is to use the client installation and look at **Help | About**, which lists the current versions of the client, engine, antivirus, and antimalware definition, and also when the policy was applied:

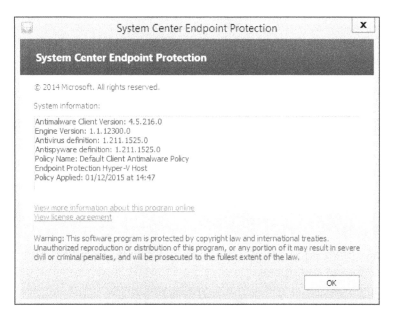

If we want to check the actual settings of the policy that are being applied, we can refer to an XML file, `%WINDIR%\CCM\EPAMPolicy.xml`, which in turn refers to the registry of the client that actually stores the policy settings. We can see these settings, including the scan schedule, exclusions and quarantine settings, in the registry at the `Computer\HKEY_LOCAL_MACHINE\SOFTWARE\Policies\Microsoft\Microsoft Antimalware` path.

We can then compare these setting to the policy as expected and defined in the Configuration Manager console. When troubleshooting policy applications, we also must consider the ordering of policies in the Configuration Manager console. It is not uncommon for administrators to misunderstand the ordering and deployment of policies, so we must check what is actually being applied from the console by looking up the relevant device in the Configuration Manager console and checking the applicable antimalware policies from the lower half of the central workspace.

In many environments, antimalware definitions will be delivered using the **Automatic Deployment Rule** feature of Configuration Manager. This should be an easy check in the console to ensure that the rule is running effectively. We can check this in the console by browsing to **Software Library | Overview | Software Updates | Automatic Deployment Rules**, where we can check the last evaluation time, last error time, and last error code. We should expect a `0x00000000` last error code, so anything other than this should be investigated using `ruleengine.log` on the site system server in the default location of `%ProgramFiles%\Microsoft Configuration Manager\Logs`. We will cover this further in the *Software Update point* section of this chapter.

Enrollment and Enrollment proxy point

These two roles are used in the process of certificate enrollment for mobile devices and the provisioning and management of Intel AMT-based computers, probably the most common usage of which is for the management of Apple Mac computers. When we talk about certificate enrollment for mobile devices, this should not to be confused with Microsoft Intune. This functionality is only related to the traditional management of mobile devices with Configuration Manager natively. We are going to discuss these two roles together as they are undeniably linked; however, in most organizations, these are likely to be separated across servers in different networks with the proxy being in a demilitarized zone. As with many other roles, these two are also web applications that run on IIS and comply to standard HTTP error codes as guidance. The default installation location for these roles are as follows:

- `%ProgramFiles%\SMS_CCM\EnrollmentPoint`
- `%ProgramFiles%\SMS_CCM\EnrollmentProxyPoint`

Troubleshooting in the console

From the console, the only area specific to troubleshooting for these roles is the standard **Monitoring** workspace where we can locate the components from **Overview | System Status | Component Status** and look at the following components:

- SMS_ENROLL_WEB
- SMS_ENROLL_SERVER
- SMS_DM_ENROLLMENTSERVICE

From here, we can check the status messages of each component and also get an indication of its current state. Using the Configuration Manager Service Manager, we can also query the current state of each service and stop or start it as required.

Troubleshooting in the log files

There are a number of log files that should be considered when trying to troubleshoot either the **Enrollment point** or **Enrollment proxy point**, and they are located in a few different folders.

By default, the %ProgramFiles%\Microsoft Configuration Manager\Logs folder contains the following log files:

- SMSENROLLSRVSetup.log
- enrollsrvMSI.log
- enrollsrv.log
- SMSENROLLWEBSetup.log
- enrollwebMSI.log
- enrollweb.log

The files named Setup and MSI will contain installation information and should be used when it is suspected that the roles have not completely installed or have been changed and are no longer functional. As always, the Setup log files will contain an overview of the installation activities and the MSI log files contain more detailed information. It should be used to identify the reason for a failed installation by verifying the return or error codes and matching them against one of the lists from the troubleshooting toolkit in *Chapter 1, The Configuration Manager Troubleshooting Toolkit*.

Then we have `enrollsrv.log`, which records the activities of **Enrollment point** or Enrollment service, as it is also known. This includes any changes to configuration, such as its SSL state and any related certificate maintenance. We will also see many references to the corresponding `web.config` file for this web application, which contains the configuration information for this role. It is not recommended to modify it directly, however; any changes to the role should be performed from within the console. This can be used as a reference though and even a comparison to a known working role in a development environment.

The log file, `enrollweb.log`, contains information on the activities of **Enrollment proxy point**, also known as the Enrollment web service. These logs should be used to confirm the availability and configuration of either of the previously mentioned site roles, and the information presented through status messages in the Configuration Manager console.

Additional to the logs already stated, there are two other log files which are by default in the following locations on the server with the roles installed:

* `%ProgramFiles%\SMS_CCM\EnrollmentPoint\Logs\EnrollmentService.log`

* `%ProgramFiles%\SMS_CCM\EnrollmentProxyPoint\Logs\EnrollmentWeb.log`

Both of these log files will confirm the starting and stopping of the web service, which should also be seen in the status messages from the console, so should be used for confirmation of any frequent outages of the roles. Additionally, `enrollmentweb.log` is the point that all devices will communicate with and so there should be a record of all communications in here if you suspect any problems enrolling a device. `enrollmentweb.log` specifically records any activity from the device—an Apple Mac for example—to the enrollment proxy point as this is the first point of communication in the enrollment chain. The log file, `enrollmentweb.log`, will then contain detailed information of the communication between **Enrollment proxy point** and **Enrollment point**. This will contain such information as enrollment attempts to include successes and failures and also certificate information used in the enrollment process.

Enrollment profiles

Additional to troubleshooting the actual installation and configuration of the roles involved in enrollment, we should also take note of the device's enrollment policy. In Configuration Manager's client settings, we can specify enrollment settings in either the default client settings policy or a custom user settings policy. Here, we specify which certificate template should be used to enroll a device, which certificate authority it comes from, and which site this enrollment profile is assigned to. Particularly in larger organizations this should be checked for changes and to ensure that the client settings' priorities are set as expected. Resultant client settings can be checked from the Configuration Manager console using the resultant client settings option from either the ribbon or the right-click menu. This is a particularly useful tool when troubleshooting application of policies and enrollment profiles for users:

Fallback status point

The fallback status point provides Configuration Manager clients with a fallback server to contact if they fail client installation, site assignment, or are unable to communicate with their HTTPS management point. We should be aware that if the fallback status point is not referenced in the client installation string using the `FSP=Server.domain.com` property then the client will not automatically use the fallback status point. The fallback status point is another low-key role that is generally installed in most environments unless there is a specific requirement not to. If someone was not involved in the initial installation of Configuration Manager, then it is possible that this role has been installed and the operator is not actually aware of it. This is another role that is hosted on IIS, and again, most common IIS troubleshooting and HTTP error codes will apply when looking into issues. The role is normally located on the default website and is a web application named `SMS_FSP`; however, unlike some other roles we have discussed, there are no files stored inside the folder for this application. There are a small number of handler mappings for the web application, similar to the management point, which in turn references system dynamic link libraries that deal with any requests made against the component. We should not need to ever change anything in the web application, but at least be aware of how the role functions in order to be able to troubleshoot it. There is no configuration required after the installation and it is normally used quite infrequently, so the scope for problems with this role is actually very limited.

Troubleshooting in the console

As with all the roles, we can start to take a look at the status of the component for the fallback status point through the Configuration Manager console using the Monitoring workspace. Browse to **Overview | System Status | Component Status** and look up the `SMS_FALLBACK_STATUS_POINT`. As with other components, this view will give us a good indicator using a color status for critical, warning, or OK. Outside of this, there isn't actually anything else in the console that we can use to troubleshoot this role as it is almost a silent technology that runs under the hood of Configuration Manager. There are a number of reports available by default which reference the data that is processed by the fallback status point. These don't necessarily directly assist us with the troubleshooting of the role other than being able to see that data is being received by the component. Should the data stop appearing then this could potentially suggest a role failure. These reports are as follows:

- Client assignment detailed status report
- Client assignment failure details
- Client assignment status details

- Client assignment success details
- Client deployment failure report
- Client deployment status details

Client deployment success report troubleshooting in the log files

As can be expected, there are a number of log files that can be used to troubleshoot the fallback status point. Located by default in `%ProgramFiles%\Microsoft Configuration Manager\Logs`, there are two log files for the installation of the role:

- `SMSFSPSetup.log`
- `fspMSI.log`

These files contain information regarding the installation and produce an exit code as with other MSI-based installers. The `SMSFSPSetup.log` file will display a return code at the end of the log file that is returned from the MSI. In turn, the `fspMSI.log` file contains output from the actual MSI installation that is somewhat more detailed, and in the case of a return or success code other than `0`, this file can be referenced to find out what the problem was.

There are a further two log files at the same location for the ongoing running of the role:

- `fspmgr.log`: This file records the day-to-day activities of the fallback status point, so any suspected problems should be first investigated within this file. It is generally a quiet log file, so anything highlighted red or yellow by CMTrace should be investigated further.
- `FSPStateMessage.log`: Finally, this is a log file located on the client by default in `%WINDIR%\CCM\Logs`. It records any state messages that are sent from the client to the fallback status point and can be used to test in isolation the functionality of the role and as a representative for other clients.

Out of band service point

Out of band management of devices, or in other words management of devices that are switched off, requires the use of the out of band service point. This role was deprecated at the introduction of Configuration Manager version 1511. We will, however, cover this as there will still be lots of people using older versions and specifically with this role installed. There are some prerequisites to using this role, however; for those that do use it, it can be very beneficial to an all-round client management approach. In order to use this role, the devices to be managed must contain Intel V-Pro chips and a version of the **Intel Active Management Technology (AMT)**. The role is very light on the server and requires the use of certificates, so as usual all standard troubleshooting applies when dealing with certificates, because these can often expire without notice and the solution stops functioning.

Troubleshooting in the console

From the console, we can obviously install the role using the standard method and we are offered the same options as are available post installation through the site system role properties. We can change the amount of retries after a failed attempt to power on an AMT-based device, the maximum number of connection threads, and also the transmission offset. These parameters are automatically set at the default and should not need changing often unless there is a specific reason by the design of the implementation. When troubleshooting, these should be given a low priority on the list of possible root causes we may have. From the site system properties, we can also supply an AMT provisioning certificate which should be created based on a very specific template set out by Microsoft. If this role is a new installation, then this is a very good check to ensure that the certificate that has been enrolled on the server is based on exactly the same template identified in the Microsoft TechNet library and must include an application policy for AMT provisioning with the object identifier of 2.16.840.1.113741.1.2.3. There is another certificate that is required for the functioning of out of band management, and this is the **AMT Web Server Certificate**. This is another template that must be created exactly as set out by Microsoft and should be checked when working with a troublesome installation. There is also a final certificate that may not be required in every implementation, which is the Client Authentication for 802.1X AMT-based computers. If we have 802.1x authentication on our network, then this should also be supplied and valid for complete out of band management.

A list of all prerequisites, both in Configuration Manager and external to it, can be found on Microsoft TechNet (`https://technet.microsoft.com/en-gb/library/gg682051.aspx`).

Additional to ensuring correct certificates and role installation, we have a set of options available through the Configuration Manager console to configure out of band management:

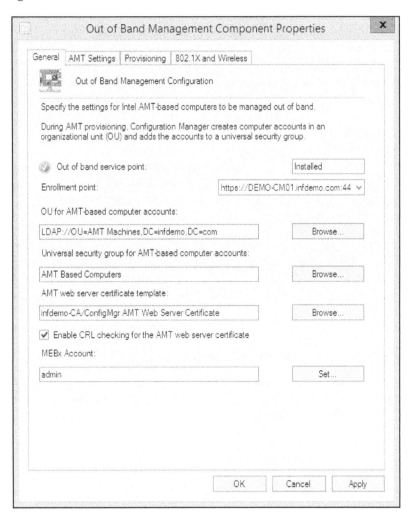

This can be obtained by looking at the **Administration** workspace in the Configuration Manager console and browsing to **Overview | Site Configuration | Sites**. Now select the relevant site from the list and select **Configure Site Components | Out of Band Management** either from the ribbon or the right-click menu. All of the information in this console window should be verified when troubleshooting as there are a number of key sections that can affect the functioning of this role. Note that CRL checking is enabled by default so we should check any relevant certificates are not revoked and that the **certificate revocation list** (**CRL**) is being successfully published by the CA. We should also take note of the MEBx account and ensure that this is still present and correct for each AMT-based computer. There is also a specific advanced setting in the **AMT settings** tab which can affect some environments and this is the Kerberos clock tolerance which by default is set to 5 minutes. In some particularly large environments there may need to be some awareness of this setting as it can sometimes fall outside of this. There are other settings in the out of band management properties that should be checked for validity, including the AMT provisioning and discovery account, the AMT provisioning removal account, and the 802.1X authentication account, where applicable. In addition to the out of band management properties, there are a small number of settings available through the site properties dialog for wake on LAN settings. It is also worth verifying these settings against expectation when troubleshooting wake on LAN-related problems specifically.

Of course, as with other roles, we can also check in the workspace and browse to **Overview | System Status | Component Status** and look up the SMS_AMT_PROXY_COMPONENT and the SMS_AMT_OPERATION_MANAGER components. As with other components, this view will give us a good indicator using a color status for critical, warning, or OK.

Troubleshooting in the log files

Looking a little deeper into the log files for out of band management we can see that there are a number of log files available in different locations that relate to the out of band service point and its functions.

In the default location of %ProgramFiles%\Microsoft Configuration Manager\ Logs folder we can find the following files:

- Amtopmgr.log (on the site system server)
- Amtproxymgr.log
- AMTSPSetup.log (on the site system server)

There is also a log file for any machines that run the out of band management console—`Oobconsole_<MachineName>_<UserName>.log`.

Additionally, there is a log file located on the client in `%WINDIR%\CCM\Logs` by default—`Oobmgmt.log`.

This role installation does not call another Microsoft installer, unlike other roles, and so the only file to look at for the installation is the `AMTSPSetup.log` file, which gives details about the registration of relevant dynamic link libraries. If there are any failures with this installation, it will be noted in the log file and the last two lines will note the unsuccessful installation. `Amtopmgr.log` holds the activities of the out of band service point, including discovery of management controllers, provisioning of AMT-based computers, control of audit logs, and also power control commands. The `Amtproxymgr.log` file holds information about communication between the site server and the out of band service point with regard to the same information as recorded in the `amtopmgr.log` file, as well as any related site replication information. Finally, the `oobmgmt.log` file is retained on the client machine and covers the AMT provisioning state of the client machine and any out of band activities on that machine.

Reporting Services point

As the name suggests, the Reporting Services point provides us with a large number of reports about our Configuration Manager installation and the clients reporting to it. It is installed in almost all Configuration Manager implementations, so we should really know how to work with this role in case of any issues. In simple terms, we are looking at a view of a Microsoft SQL Server Reporting Services instance as this is what provides the underlying technology for this role. This being the case, a certain amount of your troubleshooting may occur within SQL itself; however, there are still a number of things to check and be aware of from within the Configuration Manager console and log files.

Troubleshooting in the console

Within the console, we should be looking in the **Monitoring** workspace as this is where both our reporting and troubleshooting options will begin. It might be the case that we actually do not use the reporting from within the console and only use the Report Manager or Report Server URL, but be aware that the configuration for this is done from the Configuration Manager console. For example, if we decide to change the security in the Report Manager, we can do this, but it will be reset within 10 minutes by Configuration Manager. With this in mind, it is recommended to always stay with the Configuration Manager console when working with the Reporting Services point. We do not need to manually change any SQL Server Reporting Services settings from default when we install the role, so the likelihood is that any problems will stem from elsewhere. The most common problems are generally domain account permissions-related, and there can often be some confusion around the SQL Server service accounts and the Configuration Manager Reporting Services point account. If we have followed best practices, these should be different accounts, which should limit any confusion.

Looking in the Monitoring workspace, we can see that if we expand the Reporting node we have Reports and Subscriptions as sub-items, which most people are probably familiar with. We also see that in the results pane there are two links for the Report Manager and Report Server.

If we are experiencing problems with reporting, then this is most likely the first place to go and visit the links. This will allow us to browse the website behind the reports as mentioned earlier in this section. If these links do not respond, then there is evidently a problem contacting that site. From here we can move into the System Status and Component Status. The component we should look at is SMS_ SRS_REPORTING_POINT. As should now be familiar, we can take a high-level view of the component status from here using the **Critical**, **Warning** and **OK** status levels. If we then right-click and show all messages for this component over the previous day, for example, we should actually see limited status messages if the component is functioning normally. Assuming we are running a daily backup, these would generally consist of the status identifiers 500, 4629, and then 501, which translates to the component starting, the status summarizer detecting the availability of the component as online, and then a signaled stop of the component. These would represent a healthy Reporting Services point as far as Configuration Manager was concerned. If when running a report we find other messages, then this may well represent a SQL Server Reporting Services misconfiguration or a combination. A common problem related to configuration of the role in combination with SQL Reporting Services is the following error message:

```
"An error has occurred during report process. (rsProcessingAborted)
Cannot impersonate user for data source 'AutoGen__5C6358F2_4BB6_4a1b_
A16E_8D96795D8602_'. (rsErrorImpersonatingUser) Log on failed. Ensure the
user name and password are correct. (rsLogonFailed) Logon failure: the
user has not been granted the requested logon type at this computer"
```

There can be some variations on this specific message but it essentially refers to the account credentials that are stored in the data source in SQL. In Configuration Manager terms this is the Reporting Services Point account. In this common example the problem is usually that the account does not have the rights to log on locally as set in the corresponding **Allow log on locally** policy set in local security policy.

Troubleshooting in the log files

There are actually only a few log files which are specific to the Reporting Services point, which is perhaps surprising for something that is often used quite extensively. Furthermore, there is only one which is specific to the day-to-day working of the component, as the others are for the installation. These are located by default in the %ProgramFiles%\Microsoft Configuration Manager\Logs folder:

* SRSRPSetup.log
* SRSRPMSI.log
* SRSRP.log

The first two files listed are only relevant to the setup of the component. As is common throughout Configuration Manager setup log files, the last few lines of the `SRSRPSetup.log` file will confirm the success or failure of the component installation. The return code will correspond to the return code of the MSI used for the installation. The output from the MSI is logged into the `SRSRPMSI.log`, which gives us much more details about any failure that may have occurred. `SRSRP.log` shows information specific to the running of the reporting role, and in the case of any failure this should be referenced high on the priority list. In this log file we specifically see listed the application of security policy against the reports folder structure, so if problems are experienced with permissions to run reports, then this log file should highlight any anomalies along with any erroneous security identifiers that may be listed.

Service Connection point

This role is a new introduction into the Configuration Manager current branch, which was also known as version 1511. The role provides functionality for multiple purposes, which are as follows:

- Download of updates specific to our Configuration Manager infrastructure
- Upload of telemetry data from Configuration Manager to Microsoft
- Managing mobile devices with Microsoft Intune
- Managing mobile devices with on-premises mobile device management

Troubleshooting in the console

First of all, we should be aware that this role has only two configuration options, which are `Online` and `Offline`:

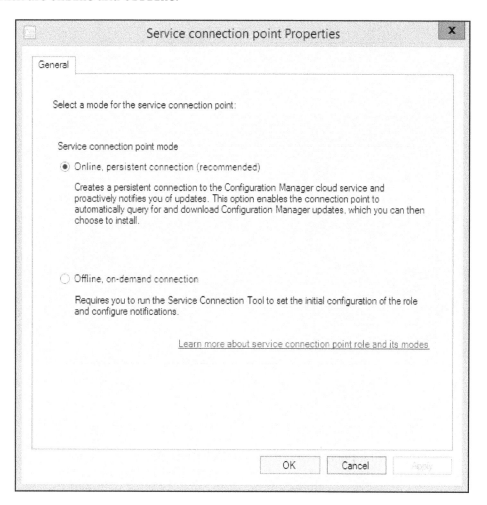

If we leave the recommended default of online, then the server will contact Microsoft every 24 hours to check for updates and upload telemetry data. The amount of telemetry data can be set by visiting the blue drop-down menu in the top left-hand corner of the Configuration Manager console. The options available are **Basic**, **Enhanced**; and **Full**.

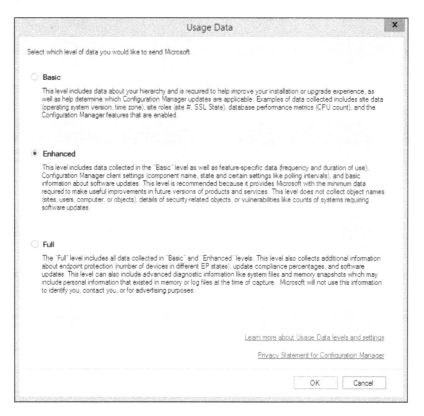

From a troubleshooting perspective, these are just about the only options in the console that we can change, and once they are set they will generally not need to be changed unless there is a specific requirement to do so. We can explore the properties of the Microsoft Intune connector in the console through **Administration | Overview | Cloud Services | Microsoft Intune Subscriptions.** Again, this is not something that we would usually need to change; however, it is worth monitoring Apple push notification certificates for expiration as this can cause real problems managing devices through Microsoft Intune. Since version 2012 R2 SP1/2012 SP2, there is an alert which will automatically notify us when the certificate is approaching expiration. We can choose how early we want to be notified, but the default value is 10 days. This is vital for retaining the functionality of managing Apple IOS devices through Intune hybrid. If the certificate expires, not only will the management of the devices cease to function, we will also have to re-enroll all relevant devices.

Troubleshooting in the log files

There are a number of log files available for troubleshooting the service connection point, which by default are available in the `%ProgramFiles%\Microsoft Configuration Manager\Logs` folder.

- `DMPUploader.log`
- `DMPDownloader.log`
- `CMUpdate.log`

The `DMPUploader.log` and `DMPDownloader.log` files should show that the upload of Intune and telemetry information to Microsoft and the download of updates to Configuration Manager and Intune through the service connection point has started. Failures will also be noted within this log file. One of the most common errors seen in these files is—`Unknown error 0x8013150C`.

This essentially means that the service connection point cannot contact the Internet to upload or download the required information. It is worth remembering with any Internet connecting role to check that the outbound connection is available, whether that is direct or through a proxy. If there is a proxy server being used, then ensure that any service accounts for authentication against the proxy are present and correct.

The `CMUpdate.log` file contains all the information about the process of updating Configuration Manager in the newer servicing model available in current branch versions of the product. Any failures will also be logged in here, and if the update process stops for some reason, then this is the log file to check and investigate from.

Software update point

The software update point is most likely to be resident in the vast majority of Configuration Manager installations around the world. In short, this role provides us with the facility to deploy software updates for Microsoft operating systems and applications in a way that gives us more control over other updating options, such as manual or Windows Server Update Services. The installation of the role is not generally too difficult but does have some particular prerequisites, depending on the version of Windows Server operating system that is running the server which hosts the role. If the role is being installed for the first time, it is important to reference the Microsoft TechNet library for the specific requirements of the relevant operating system, and therefore the version of WSUS that is being installed as part of the implementation. These can be found here—`https://technet.microsoft.com/en-us/library/hh237372.aspx`.

It is also worthwhile stepping through the procedure beforehand, as a common problem with software update point installations is that the WSUS configuration wizard is completed prior to installing the role. This then creates an error with the software update point installation, as Configuration Manager completes the configuration wizard by setting WSUS for use specifically with Configuration Manager. In addition to this there are a number of other potential pitfalls:

- Using the correct web server certificates if using HTTPS
- Configuring the correct ports for Internet access if not using a proxy or in a demilitarized zone
- Using multiple software updates points

All these things should be checked when installing the role for the first time. However, if the role is already installed, there are a number of different areas we can check to ensure the functionality of this often critical role.

Troubleshooting in the console

From the Configuration Manager console we can initially check the status of the software update point component in the Monitoring workspace. Browse to **Overview** | **System Status** | **Component Status** and look up the SMS_WSUS_SYNC_ MANAGER, the SMS_WSUS_CONFIGURATION_MANAGER, and the SMS_WSUS_CONTROL_ MANAGER components. As is now usual, we can use this to get an indication of the status of the component based on a cumulative count of status message types since 00:00. From here we can open the status message queries to reveal the error or warning messages, which will give us a good indication of any problem that exists. It is worth noting in particular with this role that sometimes problems such as a WSUS synchronization failure or an automatic deployment rule can be temporary, so a quick review of status messages is worth doing. Remember to reset the count once you are happy the role is functioning.

With this role being required for a core feature of Configuration Manager, namely software updates, there are a number of areas in the console which provide lots of information regarding the state of the role and its individual features. A quick check in the **Software Library** workspace and in **Overview** | **Software Updates** | **Automatic Deployment Rules** will show us the status of the last error on each automatic deployment rule. We can use the description as an indicator and the actual error code as something to check against an error code list from *Chapter 1, The Configuration Manager Troubleshooting Toolkit*. Additional to this, we can use the **Monitoring** workspace to check for the **Software Update Point Synchronization Status**, which lists each software update point, their catalog version, and their last synchronization status and error code.

Each piece of information can be used to indicate failure with synchronization, which can be investigated further with the relevant log files, `wsyncmgr.log` and `WCM.log`. Also, in the console we can make checks against software update product and classification selections, as this can be a problem specifically if there are multiple software update providers, such as a separate WSUS in the same domain, for example. We can look at the **Administration** workspace in the Configuration Manager console and browse to **Overview | Site Configuration | Sites**. Now select the relevant site from the list and select **Configure Site Components | Software Update Point**, either from the ribbon or the right-click menu. Here, we can check the classification and product list are as expected, and also the update languages and **Supersedence Rules**, which can often be confusing to some administrators:

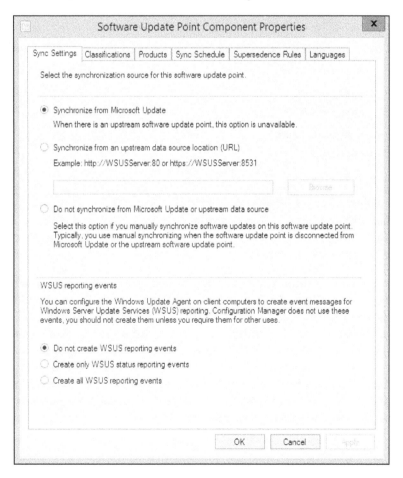

Also, if for some reason we would like to see WSUS reporting events from the WSUS console, we can amend the default selection to not create these in the software update point component properties.

Troubleshooting in the log files

As we might expect from a particularly well-consumed feature of Configuration Manager, there are quite a number of log files that can be referenced in order to troubleshoot any issues with this role.

In the default folder of `%ProgramFiles%\Microsoft Configuration Manager\Logs` we have the following log files:

- `SUPSetup.log`
- `WCM.log`
- `Wsyncmgr.log`
- `WSUSCtrl.log`

In the client in the default location of `%WINDIR%\CCM\logs` we have the following log files:

- `StateMessage.log`
- `UpdatesDeployment.log`
- `UpdatesHandler.log`
- `UpdatesStore.log`
- `WUAHandler.log`

Also on the client, we can find the `%WINDIR%\WindowsUpdates.log` file, which gives us information about what is going from the client side with regard to where the client is getting Windows updates from, and the detection and the application of updates, including any scan errors.

The `SUPSetup.log` file contains all the information around the initial installation of the role and is actually quite short, as once the wizard is complete and the prerequisites are checked it is really a process of registering dynamic link libraries. As usual, we should see an installation was successful message on the penultimate line. As briefly mentioned in the last section, when troubleshooting the software update point from the site system side we will most regularly use the `WCM.log` for information about the configuration of the role, and any misconfiguration too. This would commonly be accompanied by an error code that we can reference from one of the error code lists discussed previously.

The `Wsyncmgr.log` file is, as the name suggests, to do with the synchronization of updates from Microsoft via WSUS and can also indicate a misconfigured software update point; however, the bulk of this information is found in `WCM.log`. This log file should be checked if there is a specific issue with updates not being synchronized and the previous console checks suggest this could be at fault.

The `WSUSCtrl.log` file is more focused on the WSUS server as opposed to the Configuration Manager software update point role itself; however, it can be referenced to make checks against configuration of the Windows role, its database connectivity, and other health aspects of the WSUS server.

With software updates there is a certain amount of activity performed on the Configuration Manager client to decide which updates are applicable and then go ahead to install them and finally report back the status. As a result, there are a number of log files held on each client which can be checked on a case-by-case basis or used as a test to represent all clients if an issue is suspected to be site-wide. The `statemessage.log` file contains records of the software update state messages that are sent from the client to the management point and includes information such as the client name, version, and current user ID.

The `UpdatesDeployment.log` file is a very useful log file to check when looking into how and why updates are or are not applying to a client successfully. This file contains information about the evaluation of updates as well as the enforcement activation where applicable. Closely related, the `UpdatesHandler.log` file also contains information about the actual download of software updates and scanning for compliance against the rules set out in Configuration Manager. It is also related to `UpdatesStore.log`. `WUAHandler.log` which completes the client log files and contains records from when the client searches for software updates and bundles.

State migration point

The state migration point is another widely-used role in Configuration Manager, and in some organizations there could be one on each distribution point, so it is worth knowing where to look if this role goes wrong in any way. In very basic terms, this role is essentially a holding area for user profiles and data that has been captured from machines while they are being rebuilt. Once the machine has been rebuilt, the data is copied back down to the machine from the state migration point. All of this is done with the User State Migration tool, which should be in all Configuration Manager installations and is part of the **Windows Assessment and Deployment Kit (ADK)** and previously the **Windows Automated Installation Kit (WAIK)**. As with distribution points, we can associate state migration points with boundary groups so that Configuration Manager clients will also choose their closest state migration point, because the amount of data sent to this role can often be significant, as user profiles can sometimes be quite large. This being the case, we should use this as a first check when data is either not being saved to the state migration point or is going to the wrong state migration point. It is not unusual, particularly in larger organizations, that active directory sites or IP subnets are changed, which affects the boundaries, and the Configuration Manager administrator is often not aware of it. Another fairly common issue with state migration points is that the folder permissions are changed, either deliberately or by another tool, such as folder inheritance or even group policy. This can prevent data being stored in the folder designated in the state migration point configuration and would normally manifest itself as an HTTP 500 error. Finally, don't let the disk on which the state migration point is configured run out of space. This disk should ideally be monitored by something like Microsoft Systems Center Operations Manager. Also be realistic about the number of profiles that can be stored on the state migration point at any given time, as user profiles can sometimes be unpredictably large depending on the capture settings in the user state migration tool. A good way to prevent this is to set the deletion policy to something realistic and also cap the maximum number of clients to a reasonable amount, depending on the storage available.

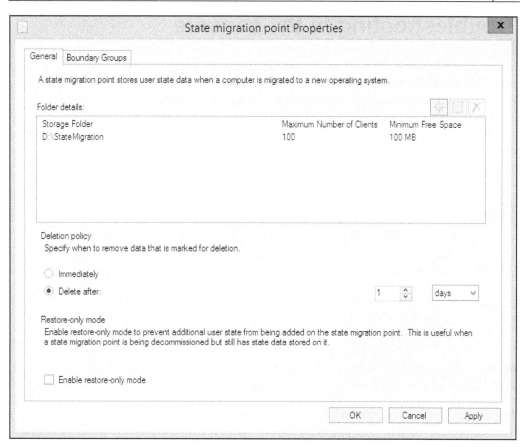

It is also preferable that any storage folders used for a state migration point are not stored on the operating system drive of a site system, as this can cause other problems if that drive becomes low on disk space.

The state migration point is another web-based application hosted on an IIS server; however, this is a virtual application and actually contains no installation files in a folder, unlike other roles. There are handler mappings configured in the SMSSMP web application that are used to work with dynamic link libraries, which are based on certain HTTP requests that include request verbs such as CCM_POST. We do not need to change any of these settings, but again it is useful to know how the role works in order to take the appropriate approach to troubleshooting.

Troubleshooting in the console

From the Configuration Manager console there is actually little that will allow us to troubleshoot this role other than the configuration we just discussed and the standard component monitoring for the Monitoring workspace. We can browse to **Overview | System Status | Component Status** and look up SMS_STATE_MIGRATION_POINT. Here, we can get an indication of the component's health and drill further into the status messages. Watch out for the **There is enough free disk on computer...** status message ID 6211, which actually reminds us that there is free space; don't get caught out like many before and misinterpret that for a negative status message.

Troubleshooting in the log files

As the state migration point is a relatively small role, there are just a handful of log files to use when troubleshooting this role. These are all located in the default location of %ProgramFiles%\Microsoft Configuration Manager\Logs:

- Smpmgr.log
- Smpmsi.log
- Smssmpsetup.log

In the %ProgramFiles%\SMS_CCM\logs folder by default we will also find the Smpisapi.log file:

The smssmpsetup.log file and the smpmsi.log file refer specifically to the installation of this role. The smpmsi.log file will give us a greater amount of detail and is the log file to refer to when there is a failed installation. If there are any failures during the MSI installation, then this will be noted in the log file with the following message:

```
Product: ConfigMgr State Migration point -- Installation operation failed.
```

From here, we can track back through the log file for more specific errors that are related to each section of the Microsoft Installer. For example, if an installation fails on the IIS prerequisite features, then a message similar to the following will be logged:

```
MSI (s) (C4!60) [09:14:24:229]: Product: ConfigMgr State Migration point -- Internal Error 25054. 80004005
```

```
CustomAction CcmValidateIISConfig returned actual error code 1603 (note this may not be 100% accurate if translation happened inside sandbox)
```

At this point, we must track back and verify the features are correctly installed against the Microsoft TechNet library here: `https://technet.microsoft.com/en-gb/library/gg712282.aspx`.

The `smpmgr.log` file contains information about the health of the state migration point and performs checks every 5 minutes to ensure that the web application is responding correctly. If at any point the role fails, then a HTTP code other than `200` should be logged here. Any configuration changes made to the state migration point are also logged here so we can tell if any amendments have been made. This is very useful, particularly if there are a number of Configuration Manager administrators working on the same servers.

Finally, the `smpisapi.log` file gives us information about the state captures and state restores that are performed and stored on the state migration point. If there are any problems with data not being stored against the state migration point, then this is a good place to check for the creation of the relevant folder.

System Health Validator Point

This role is used to validate what we define as good or bad system health when working with Microsoft Network Access Protection. This is similar to the commonly known Network Access Control, where devices are initially hosted on a remediation network to update any software, such as antivirus or operating system patches, before they are allowed onto the production or corporate network. Generally speaking, this is seldom used in Configuration Manager implementations for various reasons; however, those that do have the role installed should know where to go when trouble ensues. There are a number of prerequisites required outside Configuration Manager to run this solution, so the first check is to make sure that the network switches are configured correctly and functioning, the DHCP options are configured and functioning, and that your Microsoft Network Policy Server and Active Directory forest are in good health. A good source of information for the prerequisites and installation of this role is this Microsoft blog post: `http://blogs.technet.com/b/pauljones/archive/2013/06/02/network-access-protection-nap-with-system-center-2012-configuration-manager.aspx`.

Troubleshooting in the console

There is actually nothing to configure within the site system role itself; however, there are a small amount of settings available in the **System Health Validator Point** component properties, which can be found in the Configuration Manager console by browsing to the **Administration** workspace and looking at **Overview | Site Configuration | Sites**. Now select the relevant site from the list and select **Configure Site Components | System Health Validator Point**. Here, we can verify settings are as expected and check cross forest health state accounts are present and correct:

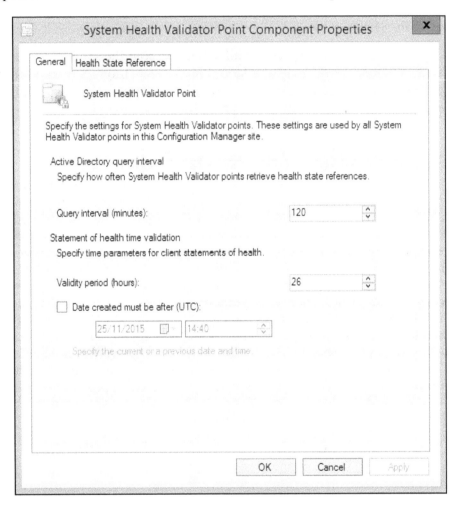

As there is so much infrastructure outside Configuration Manager for this role, the only other place we can troubleshoot within the console is by using the status message queries. If we browse to **Overview | System Status | Component Status** and look up `SMS_STATE_MIGRATION_POINT`, we can use the health indicator and open up the status messages for more specific information. A status message `1016` will signify a failed installation of the role, at which point we should start to look at the relevant log files. It should be noted that this role must be installed on the same server as the Microsoft Network Policy Server, and an inability to configure this will result in a status message code `4965`, which should be investigated further either in the log files or on the Network Policy Server itself. It is also worth noting that there are thirteen reports available by default, which includes information specific to Network Access Protection, including remediation failures, non-compliant computers, and computers where the NAP service could not be detected. These reports can be found through reporting in the **Monitoring** workspace by browsing to the category **Network Access Protection (NAP)**.

Troubleshooting in the log files

As there are several moving parts to this role there are a number of log files too. The default location for these is `%ProgramFiles%\Microsoft Configuration Manager\Logs`:

- `SmsSHVSetup.log`
- `SmsSHV.log`
- `SmsSHVADCacheClient.log`
- `SmsSHVCacheStore.log`
- `SmsSHVQuarValidator.log`
- `SmsSHVRegistrySettings.log`

On the client, we can find the following log file in `%WINDIR%\CCM\Logs` by default: `Smssha.log`.

The `SmsshvSetup.log` file, which is a small log file, details the installation and simply outputs a fairly descriptive installation code. For example, if the installation is performed on a server without the NPS Service installed, then the following will be shown in the log file:

```
Error - NPS Service is not installed on the Machine - SMSSHV Installation
cannot continue.
```

```
Installation Failed. Error Code: 131
```

- `Smsshv.log`: This file is considered to be the main log file for the daily activities of the system health validator point.

- `Smsshvadcacheclient.log`: This file details the information received about health state references from Active Directory.

- `smsshvcachestore.log`: This file holds information about the cache store and is used to store health state references that are sent from Active Directory.

- `SmsSHVQuarValidator.log`: This file contains information about the state of health from clients and how these are processed.

- `smsshvregistrysettings.log`: This file contains details of any changes that are made to the system health validator point while the service is actively running.

On the client, the log file to check is `smssha.log`, which contains lots of information, including the statement of health and exchanges with the Configuration Manager Health Agent and the Network Access Policy agent on the client operating system, as the two work together. Any failures to either validate or remediate a client's health can be checked here for errors and then investigated further in the applicable server-based log file.

Windows Intune connector

In earlier versions of Configuration Manager, this role was named the Windows Intune connector; however, as the technology was renamed and the technology developed, this role in Configuration Manager was integrated into the service connection point in the current branch or 1511 version of the product. This is the connector that brings together Microsoft Intune and Configuration Manager into a hybrid technology, partly with cloud services and partly with a traditional application to manage mobile devices, including phones, tablets and PCs. As this is primarily leveraging a cloud-based service from Microsoft, there is actually very little in the way of troubleshooting the role from a Configuration Manager point of view. Intune as a technology itself will not be covered in detail in this book as this could be a publication in itself.

Troubleshooting in the console

From the Configuration Manager console there is actually very little to change or configure other than the look and feel of the company portal and the platforms that will be supported by the role. Again, we can use the **Monitoring** workspace to check the component is up and running by browsing to **Overview | System Status | Component Status** and looking up the WINDOWS_INTUNE_SERVICE. We can open the relevant status messages from here and also query the running state and stop or start the service using the Configuration Manager Service Manager.

Troubleshooting in the log files

There are a number of log files that can be used to check the functionality of this role, and by default they are located in the %ProgramFiles%\Microsoft Configuration Manager\Logs folder on the server where the role is installed:

- Cloudusersync.log
- Dmpdownloader.log
- Dmpuploader.log
- Outgoingcontentmanager.log

The cloudusersync.log file, as the name suggests, will detail information about the Intune license enablement for users who are defined in the relevant Intune users collection. We can use this log file to check that new users added to the collection are being synchronized with Microsoft Intune and therefore being enabled for use with the service.

The Dmpdownloader.log and Dmpuploader.log file records details of any uploads and downloads to and from Microsoft Intune, including changes to the configuration, changes to the connector properties, and changes to the platform management certificates.

The Outgoingcontentmanager.log file is slightly different and details any content, such as applications, that have been uploaded to Microsoft Intune.

Summary

To summarize, this chapter has touched on all of the remaining roles with Configuration Manager, some of which are used frequently and some of which are not. The out of band service point was deprecated in the current branch of Configuration Manager, but many organizations will still use the technology and will need to troubleshoot the roles. Also, as mentioned, the Windows Intune connector was removed and its functionality was integrated into the service connection point. Some roles are covered in more detail than others, but each one should give us some pointers and places to investigate where and what to troubleshoot. Unfortunately, it is always going to be difficult to cover every single error message for every single role, but hopefully as we went through the roles, the path to a resolution should have become apparent. We can see that there is a definite path of troubleshooting from high-level information and easy access from the console down to the more specific information available in the log files, which, although they can be more difficult to read, should be made easier with the information available and tools such as CMTrace. In the next chapter, we will look into the troubleshooting of common tasks in Configuration Manager, such as application deployment and operating system deployment, as these can be common occurrences in the day-to-day management of your Configuration Manager infrastructure.

7
Troubleshooting Common Tasks

In previous chapters, we examined troubleshooting techniques for the Configuration Manager infrastructure. This infrastructure included elements such as hierarchy, site servers, site systems, and clients. It's now time to focus on some of the problems that Configuration Manager administrators face every day. In this chapter, we will examine some commonly implemented Configuration Manager features and will investigate how to resolve issues encountered during implementation.

Implementing a Configuration Manager feature can be a complicated business. There are many moving parts. Several technologies can be integrated to provide a complex solution. This is wonderful when everything works as planned. However, in the real world, problems arise. Troubleshooting when things go wrong is not always straightforward. You need to understand the various technologies and how they are integrated to work together. We will examine troubleshooting techniques for the following features:

- Troubleshooting Application Management
- Troubleshooting Software Updates Deployment
- Troubleshooting Operating System Deployment
- Troubleshooting Mobile Device Management
- Troubleshooting Certificates

Troubleshooting Application Management

Application Management is one of the most common tasks carried out by a Configuration Manager administrator. Preparation is the key to success with this feature. Remember, Configuration Manager is just the delivery mechanism. You need to research the software in advance and establish how it should be installed silently. However, despite our best efforts and forward planning, things don't always work out as we hope.

Troubleshooting steps

So what can we do when we encounter an issue? Consider the scenario. You create an application and distribute the content to your **Distribution Points** (**DPs**). You then deploy the application to a collection containing test devices. However, the application never installs. This can be daunting. What is the next step?

It's not possible for us to include every possible scenario and error code that you may encounter (use the Error Lookup component of the CMTrace tool for interpreting error codes). We have included high-level troubleshooting steps for many components in the following. More detail for some of the steps is provided later in this chapter.

Component	Troubleshooting step
Configuration Manager client	Verify that the client is healthy. The *Healthy Configuration Manager client* section in this chapter details how a healthy client should look.
	Verify that the client falls under a boundary defined in Configuration Manager. This boundary should be added to a boundary group, which is configured with one or more DPs. (**"Waiting for content"** and **"0% downloaded"** are typical messages when this is misconfigured).
	Force policy retrieval using the Configuration Manager applet in Control Panel: • Application Deployment Evaluation Cycle • Machine Policy Retrieval and Evaluation Cycle

Component	Troubleshooting step
	Examine log files for errors relating to location or site assignment: • `ClientLocation.log` • `LocationServices.log` • `ClientIDManagerStartup.log`
Client cache	Verify that the application has been fully downloaded to the client cache. Verify that the application content is less than the configured cache size (default 5 GB) (default location: `C:\Windows\CCMCache`).
Software center/ application catalog	Verify the expected behavior (see the *Application management – expected behavior* section in this chapter). Carry out a test manual installation of the application via the Software Centre.
Deployment status	Check the deployment status in the `Deployments` node of the Monitoring workspace. Applications in Configuration Manager support state-based monitoring. An application deployment has one of the following compliance states: • Success • In progress • Unknown • Requirements not met • Error
	Be aware that a failure could be reported, even though the software has been successfully installed (this would suggest a problem with the detection method).
Application	Verify that the application was created correctly. Pay particular attention to Deployment Types and Detection Methods that were manually created. Contact the application vendor for support with silent distributions.
	When troubleshooting application deployment, configure advanced logging where possible. Third-party vendors should be able to provide support for this (don't forget to disable it afterward).
	Carry out a test deployment of the application via command line (see the *Command Line testing* section in this chapter for more details). This should already be a step in your production process.

Component	Troubleshooting step
Simulated deployment	Test the deployment of an application without actually installing it on devices. The simulation evaluates the dependencies, requirement, and detection methods of a deployment. Results are displayed in the deployments node of the monitoring workspace.
Distribution point	Verify that the content has been distributed to the DP. Check the Distribution Status node of the **Monitoring workspace** | **Content Status**. Examine the distmgr.log and PkgXferMgr. log files for errors.
	Ensure that enough disk space is available to create the content. Check the SMSDPProv.log file at the remote DP.
Client Side Log files	Examine log files for errors (package/program): • CAS.log • Execmgr.log
	Examine log files for errors (application): • AppIntentEval.log • AppDiscovery.log • AppEnforce.log
Management point	Review the MP_Location.log file on the Management Point. Ensure that clients are receiving replies with DP locations.

Healthy Configuration Manager client

On the client, the Configuration Manager applet can be found in the **Control Panel**. The following screenshots show a healthy client that has received its client policy:

There are seven tabs arranged in two rows. An unhealthy client can often display six tabs arranged in a single row:

In the **Actions** tab, you can see eleven actions on a healthy client. You could see two actions on an unhealthy client. This means that the client has been installed but has yet to receive its first policy. You can read about troubleshooting the Configuration Manager client in *Chapter 3, Troubleshooting Configuration Manager Clients*.

Application management – expected behavior

For successful troubleshooting, it is important to understand the expected behavior of software deployed in the various scenarios. The following table lists available and required deployments to collections of users and devices. It describes where the user should see the status of deployed software.

Type	Collection	Deployment	Software Center	Application Catalog
Application	Users	Available deployment, no approval	After installation via Application Catalog	Yes
	Users	Available deployment, approval required	After the application is approved	Yes
	Users	Required deployment	Yes	No
	Devices	Available or required deployment	Yes	No
Package and program	Users	Available deployment	After installation via Application Catalog	Yes
	Users	Required deployment	Yes	No
	Devices	Available or required deployment	Yes	No

Command line testing

For successful Application Management, you should avoid any requirement for user intervention during the installation (with the exception of software deployed as Available). Therefore, it is important that you establish how to install the software silently from the start. Often the silent installation parameters can be found in the vendor documentation and can be of the format setup.exe /q, for example.

You should test the silent installation using the command line on a test computer. You can use **PsExec** (a component of PsTools by Windows Sys internals) to execute the process on a remote test device.

Download PsTools from the TechNet library at https://technet.microsoft.com/en-us/sysinternals/bb896649.aspx.

Remember that Configuration Manager installs software under the context of the local system account. Therefore, you must use the -s switch with PsExec to run the remote process in the System account.

Example: `psexec.exe \\testcomputer -s c:\myapp\setup.exe /q`.

This is one of the most common reasons for the failure of application deployments. If the parameters are not correct, the software can start to install but prompt for some user intervention. This is not displayed to the user as the installation is running under the local system context. The installation eventually times out and fails.

This step is normally not required where the vendor has provided an MSI file to execute the installation. Configuration Manager interrogates the MSI and is able to determine the silent installation parameters automatically. However, it is required where the vendor has provided an EXE file to execute the installation, which is rapidly becoming the norm.

Troubleshoot software update deployment

Software Updates deployment is another popular Configuration Manager feature. A robust process is essential to maintain network security and compliance. This is a complicated process consisting of many moving parts. The **Software Update Point (SUP)** is a Site System role that leverages **Windows Server Update Services (WSUS)** to make Microsoft updates available in the Configuration Manager console. The updates are then arranged in Software Update Groups and deployed using Deployment Packages. Other components used in the process include the following:

- Configuration Manager Client Agent
- Windows Update Agent (WUA)
- Device Collections
- Deadlines
- Maintenance Windows
- Automatic Deployment Rules (ADR)
- SQL Server Reporting Services

Troubleshooting steps

It's not possible for us to describe every possible issue that you will encounter when deploying a Software Updates solution with Configuration Manager. There are too many components that can be configured in many different ways. We've concentrated on the main components in the following and have added troubleshooting guidance in each case. More detail for some of the steps is provided later in this chapter.

Component	Troubleshooting step
Configuration Manager client	Verify that the client is healthy. The previous Healthy Configuration Manager client section details how a healthy client should look.
	Verify that the client falls under a boundary defined in Configuration Manager. This boundary should be added to a boundary group that is configured with one or more DPs (**"Waiting for content"** and **"0% downloaded"** are typical messages when this is misconfigured).
	Force policy retrieval using the Configuration Manager applet in Control Panel: • Machine Policy Retrieval and Evaluation Cycle • Software Update Deployment Evaluation Cycle • Software Updates Scan Cycle
	Examine log files for errors relating to location or site assignment: • `ClientLocation.log` • `LocationServices.log` • `ClientIDManagerStartup.log`
Software Update Point	Examine the `SupSetup.log` file and verify that the SUP role has been added successfully.
WSUS integration	Verify the health of WSUS using `WSUSCtrl.log`.
	`WCM.log` provides information on the SUP connection to the WSUS. Remember that WSUS could be installed on a remote server. Verify that the relevant firewall ports are open. You will find this information in the official documentation in the TechNet Library.
	Remember that you should not configure WSUS in any way. If you have, it is recommended that you uninstall and start again. Configuration Manager will configure WSUS for you.

Component	Troubleshooting step
SUP synchronization	Examine the `Wsyncmgr.log` to verify that the SUP can synchronize with the Microsoft update catalog site. When the SUP successfully synchronizes, you should see update information in the Configuration Manager console (**All Software Updates**).
	Verify that you have configured the SUP with the correct proxy credentials. In some cases, it may be necessary to whitelist the SUP on the proxy to be able to access the Microsoft Updates sites with no filtering or authentication.
	Microsoft provides an online guided walkthrough to assist in troubleshooting software update synchronization issues. It provides detailed information on known issues and difficulties which is available at `https://support.microsoft.com/en-ie/kb/2995743`.
Software Updates Group	Remember that there is a hard limit of 1,000 updates per Software Update Groups. Bear this in mind when creating your SUG structure.
	Verify that you have chosen the required products and classifications in the SUP properties.
Deployment Package	Examine the `PatchDownloader.log` file for issues in downloading updates. If you manually run the **Deploy Software Updates Wizard**, this log file will be found under your user profile in the `%localappdata%\temp` folder. This log file will only be available when updates are actually downloading.
	Verify that the deployment package has been distributed to the DP. Check the Distribution Status node of the **Monitoring workspace** | **Content Status**. Examine the `distmgr.log` file for errors.
Automatic Deployment Rules	Examine the `ruleengine.log` file for issues with ADRs. It is not uncommon to have to recreate an ADR if it is not running successfully.
Client side issues	Verify that the WUA initiates a compliance scan on the client. This compares the updates on the client to updates in the WSUS catalog. Details of this activity can be seen in `WUAHandler.log` file.
	Update the WUA to the latest version.
	Examine the following log files for issues: `UpdatesDeployment.log`, `UpdatesHandler.log`, `UpdatesStore.log`, `Wuahandler.log`, and `WindowsUpdate.log`.

Component	Troubleshooting step
	Windows 7 update scan fails resulting in client performance issues and incorrect compliance status. This is resolved with KB 3050265. It is vital that this KB is deployed
Deadlines	You should understand deadline behavior. When a deadline is reached, all required updates will start to install. However, a period of randomization of up to two hours is built into the process. Therefore, do not be alarmed if clients do not start installing updates when the deadline is reached.
Maintenance Windows	Use Maintenance Windows correctly. They are very powerful when used in conjunction with deadlines. After a deadline passes, updates will be installed as soon as the next Maintenance Windows is reached. Examine the ServiceWindow.log file for issues with this process.
Software Updates Cleanup	Clean up superseded and expired updates (see the *Software Updates Cleanup* section).
Offline servicing	Offline servicing allows you to inject updates into an OSD image file. Servicing activity is recorded in the OfflineServicingMgr.log file.

Software Updates Cleanup

Unfortunately, there is no straightforward way to manage superseded and expired updates (even in Configuration Manager 2012 R2). You still have to remove these updates manually from Software Update Groups. There is no technical reason for removing these updates. They don't interfere with the patching process. However, you can save disk space on all your servers by carrying out a regular Software Updates cleanup.

You can do this manually by using the Configuration Manager console.

1. Use the **Expired** and **Superseded** criteria search for these updates.
2. Choose **Edit Membership** to find the Software Update Groups to which they belong.
3. Uncheck the boxes and select **OK** to remove the expired and superseded updates from the selected SUGs.
4. The updates are then marked for subsequent deletion.

This process is a little tedious. PowerShell scripts are available from the Configuration Manager community, which will help you to fine-tune this process.

Troubleshoot Operating System Deployment

Operating System Deployment (**OSD**) is a very commonly used feature of Configuration Manager. It provides administrators with the necessary tools to create operating system images that can be deployed to computers. OSD troubleshooting can be a complicated process. There are so many different components and technologies working together to provide the solution:

- Windows Automated Installation Kit (AIK)
- Windows Assessment and Deployment Kit (ADK) (replacement for AIK)
- Microsoft Deployment Toolkit (MDT)
- Windows Deployment Services (WDS)
- TCP/IP Networking

Network installation of OS images is a very popular deployment method. It leverages Windows Deployment Services and ADK to provide a Pre-Execution environment, which allows for remote deployment of Windows images. Technicians press *F12* to initiate the deployment. It's very common to use the concept of *Unknown Computers* to support bare metal deployments. When you enable unknown computer support, any unknown computer can PXE boot and deploy the OSD image (note that it is useful to protect this feature with a password). If you disable this option, you can use **Import Computer Information** to prestage your computer for the OS deployment. OSD can be difficult to implement and there is a lot that can go wrong.

Troubleshooting steps

As previously stated, this is a complicated process. It is impossible to include all scenarios and error codes that you might encounter. Details of some useful troubleshooting steps are provided in the following table. Further details are provided in the following sections:

Component	Troubleshooting Step
IP Helper/DHCP Options	PXE broadcasts are not routable. If the client and PXE-enabled DP are on different subnets, you must have a method to route the PXE requests to the DP. Have you configured a solution? IP Helpers are the preferred and Microsoft-supported method. See the *IP Helper/DHCP options* section in this chapter for more details.

Component	Troubleshooting Step
Network Access Account	You must configure a network access account to use OSD in Configuration Manager. Clients use this account when they access a DP to download content required for a task sequence. If you did not configure a Network Access account, you might see the following error: `0x80070002 = The system cannot find the file specified`.
Task sequence log files	`SMSTS.log` records all the task sequence activity on the client and is the first place to look for information. Note that you will find this log file in different locations depending on the stage of the process. • WinPE, before Hard Disk Drive format: `X:\Windows\Temp\SMSTSLog` • WinPE, after HDD format: `C:\_SMSTaskSequence\Logs` • Full OS, after Configuration Manager agent installed: `C:\Windows\CCM\Logs\Smstslog` • Full OS, task sequence complete: `C:\Windows\CCM\Logs` • `Setupact.log` is the Windows installation log file. It can help you to troubleshoot installation failures. The file is located on the client (`C:\Windows\panther`).
	By default, the maximum size of `SMSTS.log` file is 1 MB. Use the `SMSTS.ini` file to increase the `LogMaxSize` parameter. Then use `DISM` to add the `SMSTS.ini` file to the boot image.
	Note that CMTrace is now included in the Configuration Manager boot images. You can use it to easily read log files while in Windows PE.
Status messages	See detailed task sequence steps through queries or reports. The following reporting categories are available using the Monitoring workspace of the console: • Task Sequence – Deployment Status • Task Sequence – Deployments • Task Sequence – Progress • Task Sequence – References See the *Task Sequence Reports* section in this chapter for more details.

Component	Troubleshooting Step
Boot image	Modify the properties of your boot images to *enable command support*. This allows you to use *F8* to open a command shell at any time during the task sequence, including while in Windows PE. Note that this should be for testing only as it is considered a security issue in production.
	The `OSDImageproperties.log` file records activity and changes to boot images.
	Both `x86` and `x64` boot images must be available on the PXE-enabled DP(even if one of them is not required for your task sequences).
	Have you selected **Deploy this boot image from the PXE-enabled distribution point** in the **Data Source** tab of the boot image properties? This is required for both `x86` and `x64` boot images.
Target computer	Note that it may be necessary to access the BIOS and enable PXE support for the Network Interface card.
	Verify network connectivity using the `ipconfig` command (use *F8* in Windows PE). Did the computer receive an IP address? Can you ping the Primary Site Server and DP?
	If the target computer does not have network connectivity, you will most likely have to import the network interface card driver into the Configuration Manager catalog and add the driver to the boot image. See the *Network Interface Card driver* section in this chapter for more details.
	Examine the `SMSPXE.log` (found on DP) file for a client request from the MAC address of your test computer. Verify that the computer receives a boot image.
PXE error	**Failed To Download Policy** (Code `0x80004005`). The PXE certificate stored in the Configuration Manager site database may have been expired. The **Time and Date** settings of the computer (BIOS) may be incorrect.
Drivers	You can find activity relating to updating or importing drivers in the `Drivercatalog.log` file.
Unknown computers	Are you are deploying OS to unknown computers? Have you enabled **Unknown Computer Support** on the DP? Search for duplicate MAC addresses.

Component	Troubleshooting Step
	The computer receives the `PXE boot file: abortpxe.com` error message. This means that there is no task sequence deployment for that device. Possible reasons: • You haven't deployed a task sequence to Unknown Computers. • You had a previous failed attempt and the computer is now *Known*. Delete Unknown computers from All Devices. • Check for duplicate computers (report). • Duplicate SMBIOS GUID (see the *Duplicate SMBIOS GUID* section in this chapter).
Task sequence	When you deployed the task sequence, did you make the deployment available to PXE (this is not the default option)?
	Check the **References** tab—is all content available on the DP?
	Verify that you are correctly partitioning the disk and that you are applying the OS image to the correct partition. `0x80070070 = There is not enough space on the disk` This is a common error and it can mean that you are trying to deploy the Windows image to the incorrect partition.
WDS issues	The WDS Server service may not be started (see the *Windows Deployment Services issues* section in this chapter).
OS deployed to D: drive	Add the `OSDPreserveDriveLetter` variable with the value `False` before the `Apply Operating System` task.
MDT integration	Additional server logging features are available (for example, **SLShare**, which copies log files centrally to a fileshare).
	Enable real-time monitoring of deployments.
Offline servicing	Offline servicing allows you to inject updates into an OSD image file. Servicing activity is recorded in the `OfflineServicingMgr.log` file.

IP Helper/DHCP options

Often you have to configure the environment to allow administrators to install operating systems on computers across the network. You need some means of allowing these computers to network boot by downloading boot images from a PXE-enabled DP(WDS server). This is easy if the computer and the WDS server are on the same subnet. The computer automatically finds the WDS server and downloads the boot image. However, the solution has to be configured to work when the computer and the WDS server are on different subnets. Some of this configuration is beyond the remit of the Configuration Manager administrator and should be carried out by the Network Administrator.

DHCP options 66 and 67 can be configured so that a PXE client can locate the WDS server and boot images. This allows a computer to boot into Windows PE. Options 66 and 67 can be configured at the server or individual scope level.

- Option 66 is configured with the name or IP address of the WDS server.

- Option 67 is configured with a filename (SMSBoot\x64\wdsnbp.com).

However, the fact that DHCP options can only be configured to find a single file can cause issues in certain cases, especially with newer **Unified Extensible Firmware Interface** (**UEFI**) computers. DHCP options are not recommended for this and other reasons. Other reasons include:

- Configuring an IP Helper on a router or layer 3 switch provides a much more reliable solution than using DHCP options.

- Using DHCP options prevents load balancing via multiple WDS servers.

- DHCP options can be configured with only a single WDS server. There is no possibility of a highly available solution.

- Clients may bypass the Windows Deployment Services answer settings.

IP Helpers (this is a Cisco term) are a much better solution to configure for network installations. They are also very easy to configure. It's quite possible that you already have IP Helpers in your network to relay DHCP requests to the DHCP server on a different subnet.

Following is an example of an IP Helper configuration on a layer 3 Cisco switch:

```
interface Vlan10
ip address 172.16.112.254 255.255.255.0
ip helper-address 172.16.1.1
End
```

This allows PXE requests from client computers in `172.16.112.0/24` subnet to find the PXE-enabled DP (`172.16.1.1`). See that the one-filename limitation does not apply here.

Network Interface Card drivers

You've tried to network boot a computer but you are unable to receive an IP address. It's likely that you will need to import a Network Interface Card driver for this computer into Configuration Manager and add this driver to the boot images. But what driver do you need to import?

The driver should be based on the installed WinPE version (which is based on the AIK/ADK version), regardless of what operating system you want to deploy.

WinPE version	AIK/ADK version	NIC driver equivalent
3.0	WAIK 2.0	Windows 7
3.1	WAIK Supplement for W7 SP1	Windows 7 SP1
4.0	ADK 8.0	Windows 8
5.0	ADK 8.1	Windows 8.1
5.1	ADK 8.1 with update	Windows 8.1 update
10.0	ADK 10	Windows 10

Finding the right NIC driver can be a trial and error process. It's better to be sure that it will work before you import and add to the boot image. Use `drvload.exe` while in Windows PE to test the driver. After you add the driver, use `ipconfig` to verify IP addressing and test connectivity using `PING`.

An example of `drvload` syntax is as follows:

- `drvload.exe E:\NIC\mynic.inf` (DRVLOAD tool temporarily adds this driver from flash drive to the WinPE boot image)
- `drvload.exe /?` (displays usage information)

When you are satisfied that you have the correct driver, you can import to Configuration Manager and add to boot images.

 Remember that only mass storage and network interface card drivers should be added to boot images.

Duplicate SMSBIOS GUID

If your solution supports Unknown Computers and there is no deployment available for your bare metal deployment, it could be that some of your new computers have duplicate SMSBIOS GUIDs. This **GUID** is configured by the vendor. If you have duplicates, you should contact the vendor for support. They may be able to provide you with a tool to reset the GUID.

You could also apply a registry change (BannedGuids) to your WDS server to prevent the detection of the duplicate GUIDs. This is not officially supported and would not be the preferred method of resolving this problem:

```
[HKEY_LOCAL_MACHINE\SYSTEM\CurrentControlSet\Services\WDSServer\
Providers\WDSPXE]
Value: BannedGuids
Type: REG_MULTI_SZ
Data: <The duplicate GUIDs>
```

Windows Deployment Services issues

WDS is automatically installed when you enable PXE on a DP in Configuration Manager 2012. You can install WDS in advance of enabling PXE but you should not configure it. Configuration Manager will configure PXE for you. This is a common mistake.

On occasions, the WDS Server service will not start. It may be necessary to disable PXE and uninstall WDS as follows:

1. Disable PXE on the DP.
2. Verify that WDS has been automatically uninstalled.
3. Reboot the server to complete the WDS uninstall.
4. Delete the RemoteInstall folder.
5. Delete all files from the C:\Windows\Temp folder.
6. Enable **PXE** on the DP.
7. Verify that WDS has been automatically installed.
8. Reboot the server to complete the WDS installation.
9. Verify that the RemoteInstall folder exists and that the smsboot folder is populated.

Troubleshoot Mobile Device Management

Mobile Device Management is a relatively new feature in Configuration Manager 2012 (introduced with Service Pack 1). The R2 version added many enhancements and the feature is growing rapidly in line with Microsoft's monthly release cadence.

The functionality is provided by adding a Microsoft Intune Subscription and Connector to your Configuration Manager site. This is a relatively new technology and the mobile device communication is carried out using a cloud service. Therefore, troubleshooting is not very advanced at this time.

Troubleshooting steps

Component	Troubleshooting Step
You have issues enrolling all devices in Microsoft Intune	This is a general problem rather than a problem with a specific component. There are a number of actions you can perform: • Recreate the Intune subscription and Intune connector. • Review the `sitecomp.log` file for errors. • Using the Configuration Manager console, verify that the `CloudUserSync` component has been created. • Check the `Dmpuploader.log` for errors relating to policy upload to Intune. • Check the `Dmpdownloader.log` for errors relating to the message download from Intune.
You cannot enroll iOS devices	Verify the **Apple Push Notification** certificate. Recreate the certificate. Shake the iOS device (while using the Intune Company Portal) to access the diagnostic log files.
You have an issue enrolling Windows 8 Phones	Ensure that the Enterprise code signing certificate has been added successfully to Configuration Manager. Re-sign the company app using this certificate.
You cannot enroll any device with a specific user	Verify the UPN of the user account. Ensure that the user account has synchronized correctly with **Azure Active Directory** (unless you are using Alternate Login IDs). Verify that the user has been discovered by Configuration Manager and that you have added them to the **Intune Users** collection (the collection configured in the Intune subscription). (See the *User Synchronization issues* section in this chapter.) Review the `adusrdis.log` file. Verify that Data Discovery Records (DDRs) are created for your users.

Component	Troubleshooting Step
Microsoft Support Request	Currently you can submit a free support request for Intune with Microsoft Customer Service and Support (CSS) (see *Microsoft Support Request* section in this chapter).

User synchronization issues

You can synchronize your Active Directory on premise user accounts to Azure Active Directory in one of the following three ways:

- Directory Synchronization Tool (DirSync) (legacy, will be deprecated)
- Azure Active Directory Synchronization Tool (AAD Sync; more advanced, replaces DirSync)
- Azure Active Directory Connect (AAD Connect; includes functionality of AAD Sync and ADFS)

The default synchronization interval for DirSync and Azure AD Sync is three hours. It can often take longer than that for the first synchronization. After a while, you may become unsure whether you have configured the solution correctly or not. Fortunately, there is a method to force the synchronization via PowerShell.

DirSync

```
C:\Program Files\Microsoft Online Directory Sync\ start-
onlinecoexistencesync
```

Azure AD Sync

```
C:\Program Files\Microsoft Azure AD Sync\Bin\DirectorySyncClientCmd.
exe
```

Selected users will be synchronized almost immediately and will be available in Azure AD within a few minutes.

While creating the Intune Subscription in Configuration Manager, you must select a user collection (for example, Intune users). Adding a user to this collection gives that user the permission to enroll mobile devices. When you add a user, you should verify that this change is synchronized to Intune using the `CloudUserSync.log` file. If the log file reports an error, you should verify that the UPN has been configured correctly on the user account.

Restart the `CloudUserSync` site component if you want the changes to be synchronized immediately. Re-examine the `CloudUserSync.log` file to ensure that the changes were synchronized to Intune.

Microsoft Support Request

Microsoft currently offer free support for any Intune-related issues (trial or production).

Local Microsoft CSS telephone numbers can be found in the TechNet Library article at `http://technet.microsoft.com/en-US/jj839713.aspx`.

You can also create an online support request via the Office 365 Admin Center. Technical Support is available in English and Japanese (nontechnical support is available in many languages).

Troubleshooting Certificates

Configuration Manager is not just a single technology that you can deploy and forget. It is a massive configuration tool with many features that can be implemented. Many different types of certificates play a role in implementing these features. We can't discuss all these certificate types in this section, but we felt we should mention some possible problems that you may encounter.

Distribution Point certificate

It is very common for the clients and servers in a Configuration Manager hierarchy to communicate via HTTP. In this case, you generally don't have to worry about securing communication via certificates. DPs are an exception. Each DP has to be configured with a least a self-signed certificate. We've previously encountered the following issues:

- The DP cannot deliver content. On examination of the DP properties, it was discovered that there was a red error icon beside the self-signed certificate. This was caused by the fact that the logged in user account was using a temporary profile when deploying the DP. When creating certificates, full access to save to the profile is required. When the profile issue was solved, the certificate could be created correctly.

- If the DP self-signed certificate expires, it must be recreated. Change the expiration date to generate a new certificate. Then you must update the boot images.

Configuration Manager and PKI

Highly secure Configuration Manager environments use PKI certificates to ensure that all traffic is encrypted (HTTPS). This is a vast and complicated area and is outside the scope of this book. We recommend the following TechNet library documents if you are having difficulty implementing this solution.

- **Planning for Security in Configuration Manager** (`http://technet. microsoft.com/en-US/ library/gg712284.aspx`)

- **PKI Certificate Requirements for Configuration Manager** (`http:// technet.microsoft.com/en-US/library/gg699362.aspx`)

- **Step-by-Step Example Deployment of the PKI Certificates for Configuration Manager: Windows Server 2008 Certification Authority** (`http://technet.microsoft.com/en-US/library/gg682023.aspx`)

Summary

In this chapter, we examined some troubleshooting steps that Configuration Manager administrators use every day. Implementing Configuration Manager features can be a complex process, and troubleshooting when things go wrong can be very daunting. When troubleshooting, it is advisable to break the process down into its component parts. We've examined the tools and techniques that will help to highlight where the problem may lie.

Configuration Manager often presents us with hexadecimal error codes when we are troubleshooting issues. Remember that these error codes can be converted to meaningful text using the Error Lookup component of the CMTrace tool.

You are never alone when troubleshooting issues. You will rarely be the first to encounter a particular issue. You can receive a lot of free support from the community by using the **Microsoft TechNet forums**.

In the next chapter, we will discuss Configuration Manager Disaster Recovery. We will examine some scenarios for recovering sites when all troubleshooting attempts are in vain.

8
Disaster Recovery

A book on Configuration Manager troubleshooting would not be complete without reference to **Disaster Recovery** (**DR**). What do you do when all else fails? Many administrators will never have to recover Configuration Manager in this way. However, they must be prepared for the worst-case scenario. It's a very important aspect of our job.

So what is DR? In simple terms, it is the ability to recover a service from catastrophic failure in the least possible time with minimal data loss. A **Disaster Recovery Plan** (**DRP**), sometimes known as a **Business Continuity Plan**, documents the procedures and policies required to recover services. You (or one of your team) are responsible for the Configuration Manager DRP.

So what has to be done? What does DR mean in relation to Configuration Manager? Infrastructures vary across organizations. Some have large environments with a Central Administration Site and several Primary Sites. Recovery techniques for these organizations may differ from organizations with a single Primary Site. In this chapter, we will discuss DR solutions. It is not meant to be a comprehensive walk-through for implementing a DR solution. Rather, it will give you an overview of what is required.

- Planning for Disaster Recovery
- Robust backup process
- Configuration Manager Site Restore
- High availability

Planning for Disaster Recovery

Make no mistake. Recovering from a Configuration Manager failure is a complex process. You must be skilled with the product and the integrated components. The process must be well planned in advance. All the information you need should already be available. The next section describes some of the items you should consider.

Document your environment

As a Configuration Manager administrator, you should document your environment thoroughly. Of course, this isn't just part of a DR process. It's just common sense. However, in reality, this is not always the case.

1. Start by drawing a diagram of the hierarchy (very large environments may have a CAS, multiple Primary Sites, and, perhaps, multiple Secondary Sites).

2. Illustrate the hierarchy accurately, even if you only have a single Primary Site.

3. Include the server names in the hierarchy diagram.

4. Create a table containing all the information you are likely to need for recovery of each Site System. Don't worry if you think you have too much information. In terms of information and DR, it's better to be *looking at it* than *looking for it*.

A typical table for a single Primary Site could be as seen in the following (note that the specifications are examples, not recommendations):

	SERV01	**SERV02**
Physical or virtual	Virtual	Virtual
Server specification	16 GB RAM 2vCPU	4 GB RAM 2vCPU
High availability	Yes, at Hypervisor level	No
Role(s)	Primary Site Server Management Point Database Software Update Point Reporting Services Point Intune Connector	Management Point Distribution Point Software Update Point

	SERV01	SERV02
Configuration Manager version (including SPs and CUs)	Configuration Manager 2012 R2 SP1 (5.00.8239.1000)	
Site code	P01	P01
Operating system	Windows Server 2012 R2 (6.3.9200)	Windows Server 2012 R2 (6.3.9200)
Drive partitions (examples)	C: 80GB (OS) E: 80GB (Program files) F: 80GB (Database) L: 30GB (Log files) T: 30GB (Temp DB)	C: 80GB (OS) E: 80GB (Program files) F: 200GB (Content Library)
Domain	MyDomain.local	MyDomain.local
Configuration Manager installation folder	E:\Program Files\Microsoft Configuration Manager	
SQL Server information	Local SQL Server 2012 SP2 CU4 (11.0.5569.0)	

You may have spotted a reference to High Availability (HA) in the table. Configuration Manager is not a *real-time* product and a certain amount of downtime can be tolerated in most cases. However, it is still beneficial to build as much redundancy into the solution as possible to try and eliminate, or at least minimize, the requirement for DR. HA is discussed later in this chapter.

Create Disaster Recovery Plan

A DRP details everything you may need to recover the service after a catastrophic failure. The DRP will include at least the following items:

- Documentation describing the environment (diagrams of infrastructure, tables containing Site System information).

- Documented backup processes (see the *Robust backup process* section later in this chapter for more details).

- Documented recovery processes (see the *Configuration Manager Site Recovery* section later in this chapter for more details).

- Checklist for testing after site recovery (this should be a comprehensive list of tests to verify that all features are functioning as they did previously).

- Results from previous DR tests (which should include what was learned from previous tests). Regular DR tests should be carried out in a lab environment.

The DRP should be *live* and should be updated whenever major changes are made to the Configuration Manager environment.

> Note that DR testing is not easy with Configuration Manager. As restored servers generally need to have the same name as the original server, it is not possible to test in production. The only way to test DR properly is to duplicate the production environment as best you can on an isolated network.

When you carry out your DR tests, you should record how long it takes for full recovery. This is an important piece of information to be able to share with management when you are looking for approval of your DRP.

Robust backup process

In Configuration Manager 2007, there was only one method to back up and restore your site. You had to configure a built-in maintenance task (**Backup Site Server**). Configuration Manager 2012 now supports two methods of recovery. You can still use the traditional maintenance task method. However, you can also recover your site from an SQL database backup. This is now the preferred method and has a number of advantages over the maintenance task.

- The maintenance task backup will copy all of the database data and log files to the backup folder location, whereas you can compress the backup files using the SQL backup. This could lead to a huge saving in disk space.

- When you use the SQL backup task, you can take advantage of advanced features such as retention periods and integrity checks.

- The maintenance task backup first stops Configuration Manager Services before copying the database data and log files. This is not the case with the SQL backup, which causes no service downtime.

There is, of course, an obvious advantage to using the built-in maintenance task backup. Many organizations employ both dedicated Configuration Manager administrators and dedicated Database administrators. In these cases it, may be more useful to implement the maintenance task solution. In this way, the Configuration Manager administrators will have more visibility and control of the backup process rather than relying on the other team.

Choose the option that will work best for you. Then you must ensure that you have a robust backup process. You must regularly check the backup status and carry out test restores as stated in your DRP.

Note that you could choose to implement both backup solutions. There are no adverse effects to doing this, providing the backups are scheduled so that they don't overlap. This gives you more options when it comes to recovering a site.

The following sections describe the high-level tasks required to implement each of the supported Configuration Manager backup methods.

Maintenance task backup

Using the Configuration Manager console, navigate to **Administration | Site Configuration | Sites**. Right-click on your site and choose **Site Maintenance**. You are presented with a list of maintenance tasks for the site. **Backup Site Server** is the first of these tasks, as shown in the following screenshot:

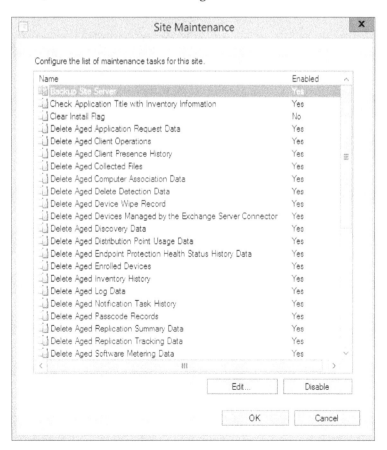

This section describes the steps required to enable this maintenance task.

1. Create a network shared folder to store the backup files. Within the shared folder, create a folder for each server that is to be backed up.

2. Configure the required NTFS permissions on the folder. The computer account of the site server and the computer account of the SQL Server require **Write** permissions.

3. Configure the required **Share** permissions on the folder. The computer account of the site server and the computer account of the SQL Server require **Change** permissions.

4. Open the **Site Maintenance** dialog box as described previously.

5. Choose **Backup Site Server** and click on **Edit.**

6. Select **Enable this task**.

7. Click on **Set Paths** and browse to a location to store the backup files. Although you can choose a local folder, it is recommended to choose the previously created network share. Use UNC path.

8. Configure the backup **Schedule**. Choose the required frequency and start time. Note that it is considered best practice to run backups outside normal working hours.

9. Choose **Enable alerts for backup task failures** (optional).

10. Apply the changes.

11. Verify your configuration with a manual backup. Start the SMS_SITE_BACKUP service (this service is configured for manual start).

12. Review the Smsbkup.log file for errors.

13. Examine the backed up files in the network share. Note the SiteDBServer and SiteServer folders. The SiteDBServer folder contains the CM_sitecode.mdf and CM_sitecode_log.ldf files.

14. Note that you can optionally run an after backup batch file, which performs archiving and other administrative functions. The AfterBackup.bat file should be placed in the <ConfigMgrInstallationFolder>\Inboxes\Smsbkup.box folder.

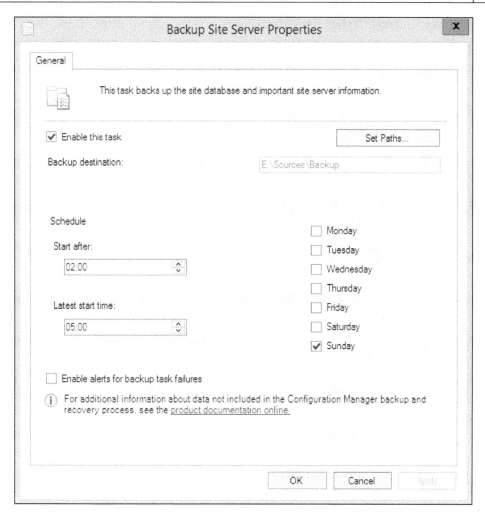

SQL backup

Follow these high-level steps to implement the SQL Backup using the SQL Server Management Studio:

1. Open **SQL Server Management Studio** and connect to the **Configuration Manager SQL** instance.

2. Navigate to **Management | Maintenance Plan**.

3. Right-click on **Maintenance Plan** and select the **New Maintenance Plan Wizard**.

4. Click on **Next** to start the wizard.

5. Enter a suitable name and click on **Change** to configure a schedule.

6. Configure the backup **Schedule**. Choose the required frequency and start time.

 Note that it is considered best practice to run backups outside normal working hours.

7. Click on **OK** to save the schedule and then click on **Next** to continue.

8. You are presented with a list of maintenance tasks to choose from. It is recommended to choose **Clean Up History**, **Back Up Database (Full)** and **Maintenance Cleanup Task**.

9. Click on **Next** to continue to the **Define History Cleanup Task**.

10. It makes no sense in Configuration Manager to restore an old database. Therefore, we can configure **Remove historical data older than** to be 1 week. Ensure all historical data items are selected.

11. We are now presented with the **Define BackUp Database (Full) Task** dialog box. Use the drop-down arrow to select the databases you want to back up.

12. Select the required remote location for the backup. It's good housekeeping to **Create a sub-directory for each database**. Choose to **Compress Backup**.

13. In the **Define Maintenance Cleanup Task** dialog box, configure the previously configured backup folder. Configure BAK as the **File extension** (note that you must enter bak, not .bak).

14. Check the **Include first-level folders** and **Delete files based on the age** boxes. Choose 1 week for the age. Click on **Next** to finish.

15. Manually run the maintenance plan and verify success.

16. Verify that the database has been successfully backed up to the remote location.

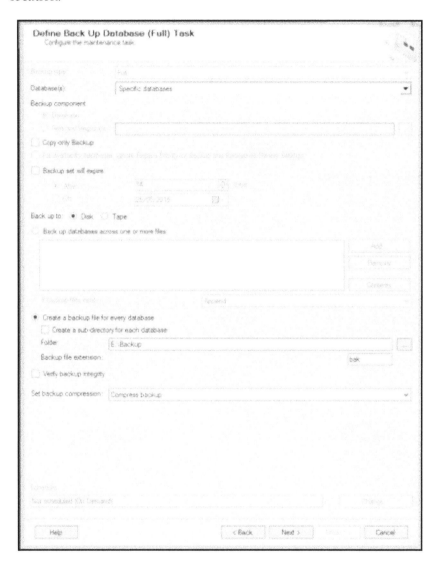

Additional items to be backed up

The previous sections described the two methods for backing up a Configuration Manager site. The SQL backup utilized an SQL Maintenance Plan to back the SQL database and log files. The Backup Site Server maintenance task provides a backup for the site database and some additional site server files. However, there are other important items that are not backed up using either method. These must be considered when planning your backup strategy.

The following items should be backed up using your organization's standard backup procedures.

Content Library

The Content Library was introduced in Configuration Manager 2012 to optimize disk storage and to avoid distributing files to DPs if they already exist. A copy of the *single-instance store* is kept on the site server as the source for the distribution points. You must manually back up the Content Library as it is not automatically included in any of the previously discussed methods. It must be restored before you will be able to redistribute any content to the DPs. When you redistribute content in Configuration Manager, the files are copied from the Content Library on the site server to the DPs.

The SCCMContentLib folder on the site server is the content library location. It's normally found on the disk drive, which has the most available space when the site is installed.

The following folders should be backed up:

- SCCMContentLib
- SMSPKG
- SMSPKGSIG
- SMSSIG$ (Primary Site only)
- SMSPKGX$ (where X is the drive letter – Primary Site only)
- Source files

It is good practice to locate the package source files on a highly available remote share. Regardless of the location, they are very important and should be included in every organization's backup routine. The source files must be restored to allow you to update content on DPs. After any content update, Configuration Manager first copies the updated files from the source location to the content library. The updated content is subsequently copied to the DPs.

SQL Server Reporting Services (SSRS)

There are some actions required in order to facilitate the recovery of SSRS:

- Back up encryption keys using the Reporting Services Configuration tool.

- Back up reporting services configuration files typically found in `\Program Files\Microsoft SQL Server\MSRS11.MSSQLSERVER\Reporting Services` (see the list in the following table).

- Back up `ReportServer` and `ReportServerTempDB` databases. This is very straightforward using the SQL Maintenance Plan previously discussed.

Reporting services configuration files:

Filename	Path
Rsreportserver.config	\Program Files\Microsoft SQL Server\ MSRS11.MSSQLServer\Reporting Services\ReportServer
Rssvrpolicy.config	\Program Files\Microsoft SQL Server\ MSRS11.MSSQLServer\Reporting Services\ReportServer
Rsmgrpolicy.config	\Program Files\Microsoft SQL Server\ MSRS11.MSSQLServer\Reporting Services\ReportManager
ReportingServicesService.exe. config	\Program Files\Microsoft SQL Server\ MSRS11.MSSQLServer\Reporting Services\ReportServer\bin
RSWebApplication.config	\Program Files\Microsoft SQL Server\ MSRS11.MSSQLServer\Reporting Services\ReportManager

Software updates

After you have recovered your Configuration Manager site, you will have to recreate your software updates solution. At that point, we would recommend deploying the solution from scratch rather than restoring the solution from backup. However, as both methods are valid, we should discuss the backup/restore method. You will need to carry out these steps to be able to restore from backup:

- Backup SUSDB using the SQL Maintenance Plan previously discussed. Note that you can also use SQL Backup to back up the database even if you have configured your solution to use the Windows Internal Database.

- Don't forget to also back up the WSUS folder that you created when you added the role.

Please note the following:

- If you are using System Center Updates Publisher 2011 (SCUP) for deploying third-party updates, it is recommended that the solution is recreated from scratch.

- If you recreate the software updates solution from scratch (recommended), you will also have to recreate the Endpoint Protection solution.

VM snapshots

 It's very important to note that virtual machine snapshots should not form part of a DR solution. Sites that are part of a hierarchy should never be restored by using a snapshot. Even if the site looks healthy initially, you may encounter difficulties later on.

Snapshots are a very useful feature that we can use in our everyday management of virtual machines (VMs). A snapshot allows an administrator to roll back a VM to a previous state. This allows you to undo recent changes and sounds wonderful. However, you need to know how to use snapshots properly.

Creating a snapshot actually creates another virtual hard disk file. This differencing disk stores the differences that would normally be written to the original virtual hard disk. The differencing disk grows in size as long as the snapshot remains. This process fragments the drive and can affect VM performance.

Snapshots should seldom be used and only as a temporary measure when you are carrying out a risky operation. You can revert if the operation fails. If you don't need the snapshot after the operation has been completed, then you should merge and remove the snapshot. Snapshots are for temporary use and are not a substitute for a robust DR solution.

You have been warned.

Troubleshooting backup failures

As we discussed earlier in this chapter, the SQL maintenance plan backup is the recommended backup solution for the Configuration Manager site. You will see later that you can fully recover the site as long as you can restore the SQL database. The Configuration Manager maintenance task backup is still valid and widely used but can be the most problematic of the two.

Following are some tips for troubleshooting backup issues:

- Log files:
    - ° Review `SMSBKP.log` and `smswriter.log` file for errors.

- Remote Share Permissions:
    - ° Check that you have configured the correct permissions if you have configured the backup to write to a remote share. The computer account of the site server (and SQL server if remote) requires write/delete permissions on the share.
    - ° Use `psexec.exe` in system context in order to test the permissions.
    - ° Execute a backup locally for testing purposes.

- Services:
    - ° Verify that the following automatic services are started: `SMS_SITE_VSSWriter`, `SMS_SITE_SQL_Backup`
    - ° `SMS_Site_Backup` is a manual service. Can you start the service?

- Known issue with remote share:
    - ° If you back up directly to a remote share, you may encounter errors such as **The backup folder does not exist** or **The backup service does not have permission to access the folder**. This is a known issue. Create a folder within share and configure the backup to use that folder.

Configuration Manager Site Recovery

Previously, in this chapter, we've discussed the different Configuration Manager backup options. Now let's have a look at how these backups can be used to recover sites and site servers in case of a disaster. There are multiple ways to recover a site. The method you can use depends on what has happened and what backup is available to you.

We will concentrate on the following four possible scenarios in this chapter:

- Install new Configuration Manager Primary site and restore previous site from SQL backup.
- Install new Configuration Manager Primary site and restore previous site from Configuration Manager backup.
- Recover Primary site from Configuration Manager backup.
- Recover Secondary Site.

In order to see what options there are, launch the **Configuration Manager Setup Wizard** using `splash.hta` on the installation media. Choose **Recover a Site** from the **Available Setup Options**. You are presented with the **Site Server and Database Recovery Options** dialog box.

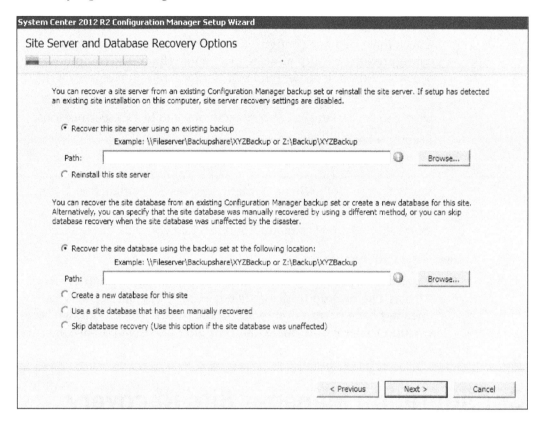

Recovery options

Here you can see the available recovery options. There are two sections, each with a number of options.

Recover a Site Server

The first section is for recovering or reinstalling a site server. This section is disabled if setup detects an existing site. The options are as follows:

- **Recover this site server using an existing backup**
- **Reinstall the site server**

Recover a Site Database

The second section allows you to choose database options. The options are as follows:

- **Recover the site database using the backup**
- **Create a new database for this site**
- **Use a site database that has been manually recovered**
- **Skip database recovery (Use this option of the site database was unaffected)**

Prerequisites

Recovering a Configuration Manager site server requires the same prerequisites that we needed when installing for the first time. We need to ensure that all prerequisites are in place. Some prerequisites depend on what Configuration Manager features you use in your environment, but if you've documented your site well, you will be able to see at a glance what you need.

Typical prerequisites are as follows:

- Install the required Operating System and fully update
- Use the same server name as previously (recommended)
- Use the same drive partitions as previously (recommended)
- Windows Assessment and Deployment Kit (ADK)
- IIS with specific role services
- Background Intelligent Transfer Service (BITS)
- Remote Differential Compression
- .NET Framework
- Windows Server Update Services (WSUS—installed but not configured)
- Windows Deployment Services (WDS—installed but not configured)
- SQL Server (if SQL was installed locally on the site server before the disaster)
- Configure SQL with the same instance name as previously

Install Primary Site and restore database from SQL backup

In this first example, we will create a new Primary Site with the same sever name and site code as previously used. Then we will delete the new Configuration Manager database and restore from SQL backup. Finally, we will run through the recovery setup choosing the newly restored database.

The high-level steps here describe the recovery process:

1. Install a new **Primary Site** as normal (same server name and site code).
2. Install the same hotfixes as previously.
3. Launch **SQL Server Management Studio** and delete the Configuration Manager database.
4. **Restore** the previously backed up Configuration Manager database using SQL Server Management Studio.
5. Launch **Configuration Manager Setup Wizard** using `splash.hta` on the installation media.
6. **Choose Recover a Site** from the **Available Setup Options**.
7. You are presented with the **Site Server and Database Recovery Options** dialog box. Note that **Recover site server** will be grayed out as Configuration Manager has already been installed.
8. Choose **Use a site database that has been manually recovered**.
9. In **Site Recovery Information** dialog box, ensure **Recover Primary Site** is selected and click on **Next** (there is no CAS in this environment).
10. The next few dialog boxes will be familiar to you as a regular installation (Product key, license terms, prerequisite downloads).
11. The **Site Code** and **Site Name** will be prepopulated in the **Site and Installation Settings** dialog box. Verify the installation folder and choose to **Install the Configuration Manager console**.
12. Verify the prepopulated **SQL database** name.
13. Configure the drive locations for the SQL database and log files.
14. Review the **Settings Summary** and ensure that you are satisfied with your choices.
15. The **Prerequisite Check** runs (hopefully with success).
16. Select **Begin Install** to commence the Site Recovery.
17. After the site is recovered, re-enter the passwords and install the hotfixes requested by the wizard.

Install Primary Site and restore database from Configuration Manager backup

This scenario is slightly different. We do not have an SQL database backup but we have used the Configuration Manager backup solution. In this case, we will create a new Primary Site with the same sever name and site code. Then we will delete the new Configuration Manager database and recover the site using the Configuration Manager Recovery Wizard:

1. Install a new **Primary Site** as normal (same server name and site code).

2. Install the same hotfixes as previously.

3. Launch SQL Server Management and delete the Configuration Manager database.

4. Launch **Configuration Manager Setup Wizard** using `splash.hta` on the installation media.

5. Choose **Recover a Site** from the **Available Setup Options**.

6. You are presented with the **Site Server and Database Recovery Options** dialog box. Note that **Recover site server** will be grayed out as Configuration Manager has already been installed.

7. Choose **Recover the site database using the backup set at the following location** and enter the location of the Configuration Manager backup.

8. The wizard interrogates the backup files and presents you with your recovery options in the **Site Recovery Information** dialog box. Click on **Next** as there is no CAS in this environment.

9. Again, the next few dialog boxes should be familiar to you (Product key, license terms, prerequisite downloads).

10. The **Site Code** and **Site Name** will be prepopulated in the **Site and Installation Settings** dialog box. Verify the installation folder and choose to **Install the Configuration Manager console**.

11. Verify the prepopulated **SQL database** name.

12. Configure the drive locations for the SQL database and log files.

13. Review the **Settings Summary** and ensure that you are satisfied with your choices.

14. Click on **Next** to run the **Prerequisite Checker**.

15. Review any errors or warnings.

16. Select **Begin Install** to commence the Site Recovery.

17. After the site is recovered, re-enter the passwords and install the hotfixes requested by the wizard.

Recover Primary site from Configuration Manager backup

In this example, the site server and site database will be recovered using the Configuration Manager backup. We do not install Configuration Manager in advance. The steps here describe the recovery process:

1. At the **Site Server and Database Recovery Options** dialog box, choose the following options. Enter the location of the backup files.

    ° **Recover this site server using an existing backup**

    ° **Recover the site database using the backup**

2. The wizard interrogates the backup files and presents you with your recovery options in the **Site Recovery Information** dialog box. Click on **Next** as there is no CAS in this environment.

3. The next few dialog boxes will be familiar.

4. The **Site Code** and **Site Name** will be prepopulated in the **Site and Installation Settings** dialog box. Verify the installation folder and choose to the **Install the Configuration Manager console** option.

5. Verify the prepopulated **SQL database** name.

6. Configure the drive locations for the SQL database and log files.

7. Review the **Settings Summary** and ensure that you are satisfied with your choices.

8. The **Prerequisite Check** runs (hopefully with success).

9. Select **Begin Install** to commence the Site Recovery.

10. After the site is recovered, re-enter the passwords and install the hotfixes requested by the wizard.

Recover Secondary Site

Recovering a Secondary Site is very straightforward. This operation can be carried out using the Configuration Manager console and you don't even need a backup. The procedure is as follows:

1. Install server Operating System. Choose the same name as the previous Secondary Site server.

2. Add Primary Site server computer account to the local administrators group of the new secondary site server.

3. Give the new secondary site server full control of the System Management container.

4. Install prerequisite roles and features (IIS, BITS, Remote Differential Compression, .NET Framework).

5. Install the same version of **SQL express** that you had before the disaster. Use the same instance name.

6. In the Configuration Manager console, navigate to **Administration | Site Configuration | Sites**. Select the Secondary Site and choose **Recover Secondary Site from the ribbon above**.

7. The secondary site is recovered directly from the parent primary site.

Additional items to be restored

In the previous *Additional items to be backed up* section of this chapter, we discussed the fact that there were other important items that were not backed up using either SQL backup or the Configuration Manager maintenance task. These items had to be backed up using a separate process and therefore have to be restored separately after recovering a CAS or Primary Site server.

Content library

The following folders should be restored. They have to be restored to the same drive and path as the original server.

- SCCMContentLib
- SMSPKG
- SMSPKGSIG
- SMSSIG$ (Primary Site only)
- SMSPKGX$ (where X is the drive letter – Primary Site only)

You will also need to recreate IIS directories using the Configuration Manager console as follows:

1. Navigate to **Administration | Site Configuration**.
2. Choose the server you have just restored.
3. Select the **Distribution Point Site System** role and choose **Properties**.
4. Check the **Allow clients to connect anonymously** box and click on **Apply**.
5. Verify that the virtual directories have been recreated in IIS Manager.
6. Review the `distmgr.log` file to see that the directories have been created successfully.
7. Once you have verified the new directories, you can uncheck the **Allow clients to connect anonymously** box and click on **Apply**.

This process recreates the following IIS directories:

* `SMS_DP_SMSPKG$`
* `SMS_DP_SMSSIG$`

Source files

The source files must be restored to allow you to update content on DPs in the future. The files must be restored to the same location as they were on the original site server.

SQL Server Reporting Services (SSRS)

The high-level steps for restoring SSRS are as follows:

1. Ensure that you have previously installed SQL Server Reporting Services.
2. Navigate to **Administration | Site Configuration**.
3. Choose the server you have just restored.
4. Choose to **Add Site System Role** and add the **Reporting Services Point**.
5. Using SQL Management Studio delete the existing Reporting Services Databases (**ReportServer** and **ReportServerTempDB**).
6. Restore the **ReportServer** and **ReportServerTempDB** databases from backup.
7. Restore the reporting services configuration files (these files were listed in the previous *Additional backups* section).
8. Use Reporting Services Configuration Manager to restore the Encryption key from backup.

Software updates

1. Add the WSUS role as normal.

2. Complete the initial WSUS configuration and choose a folder for the WSUS metadata. Ensure that this folder is on the same location as on the original site server.

3. Using SQL Management Studio, restore the WSUS database (SUSDB) from backup. Ensure that the database has been restored to the same location as on the original site server.

4. Ensure that WSUS certificates are correctly created.

5. Distribute WSUS certificates to Configuration Manager clients.

6. Synchronize software updates.

7. Review `Wsyncmgr.log`, `WSUSCtrl.log`, and `WCM.log` for errors.

Testing

A Configuration Manager site consists of several components and relies on many different technologies. After you recover the site, you will have to carry out extensive testing to verify that the functionality is the same as before. A checklist for testing should be included in your DRP.

So what should be included in the checklist? The following table shows some of the items that you should test:

Component	Test
Management Point(MP)	Verify that the Management Point is responding to client requests. Test by using these URLs from some test clients: • `http://<MP_name>/sms_mp/.sms?autMPCERT` • `http://<MP_name>/sms_mp/.sms?autMPLIST` If the MP does not respond successfully, you can safely remove the role and reinstall it. Refer to *Chapter 5, Troubleshooting Management Points and Distribution Points*, for more details.

Component	Test
Client	Verify that clients are now receiving policies from the restored MP. Using the Configuration Manager applet in **Control Panel**, force the **Machine Policy Retrieval & Evaluation Cycle**.
	Review the `PolicyAgent.log` file for errors.
	Using the Configuration Manager console, test the client remote control feature. This is a good test for testing client functionality.
	Refer to *Chapter 3, Troubleshooting Configuration Manager Clients*, for more details.
Distribution Point	Verify that the solution can handle content. Create a new package and distribute it to the DPs.
	Review the `distmgr.log` file for errors.
	Refer to *Chapter 5, Troubleshooting Management Points and Distribution Points*, for more details.
Software Distribution	This is a good test for testing end-to-end functionality. Use the package that you created previously and deploy it to a test collection of devices. Verify that the behavior is as expected (available/required, Software Center/Application Catalog).
	See the *Troubleshooting Software Distribution* section of *Chapter 7, Troubleshooting Common Tasks*, for details of this expected behavior.
Operating System Deployment (OSD)	OSD testing includes all the items already mentioned previously. Additional tests are as follows: • Check that computers can PXE boot and receive policy to select a task sequence. • Verify that OSD task sequence completes successfully. • Verify that Configuration Manager client is healthy after OSD task sequence. Refer to *Chapter 7, Troubleshooting Common Tasks*, for more details.
Software Updates	Verify that Configuration Manager can still synchronize with the Microsoft Update catalog. Check that Software Update Groups can be created and that updates can be downloaded to Deployment Packages.
	Finally, ensure that updates are installed on clients where required.
	Refer to *Chapter 7, Troubleshooting Common Tasks*, for more details.
Hardware Inventory	Check that Configuration Manager clients are able to send hardware inventory information to the Management Point. Use Resource Explorer, queries, and reports to verify this.

High Availability

We previously mentioned that Configuration Manager is not a *real-time* product and a certain amount of downtime can be tolerated in most cases. However, it's also useful to add HA to the solution where possible as this would reduce the risk of having to recover a site using the techniques that we described in this chapter.

It's important to note that we cannot implement fault tolerance for all Configuration Manager roles. This section describes some important roles and highlights whether or not it is possible to introduce HA.

- **Site Server**: Main site system role. The Site Server hosts the Configuration Manager components and services. *There are no HA options.*

- **Site Database Server**: hosts the Configuration Manager Site Database. *SQL can be installed in a HA cluster.*

- **SMS Provider**: WMI provider used to access and modify Configuration Manager data. *You can install multiple SMS Providers.*

- **Management Point**: Accepts management data and replies to requests from Configuration Manager clients. *You can install multiple Management Points.*

- **Distribution Point**: Stages packages for distribution to clients. *You can configure alternative and fallback DPs.*

- **Software Update Point**: Role required to implement a software updates solution. *You can install multiple Software Update Points.*

Summary

In this chapter, we dealt with DR in Configuration Manager. We discussed the importance of planning for DR and how to create the DRP. Don't forget to update the information in the plan as your infrastructure changes. We explained that there are two backup methods available to you and recommended that you implement a solution using SQL backup.

Let's hope that you don't have to recover a Configuration Manager site any time soon but we described some scenarios that you could encounter and how you should restore the site and additional required items.

The recovery of site systems that are configured to communicate via HTTPS is outside the scope of this book. However, it should be noted that you must reconfigure IIS to use the web server certificate after you recover these systems. In the next chapter, you are going to learn high-level good practices for the administration and maintenance of Configuration Manager. It will list some tasks that can be used on regular interval periods to aid the user in avoiding having to troubleshoot Configuration Manager at all or at least make troubleshooting easier.

If you require additional information, please review the official product document **Backup and Recovery in Configuration Manager** at `https://technet.microsoft.com/en-us/library/gg712697.aspx`.

In the final chapter, we will discuss tips to avoid getting into trouble in the first place. This is always better than having to troubleshoot when things go wrong.

9

Avoiding Trouble

We examined Configuration Manager troubleshooting techniques in the previous chapters. These techniques ranged from solving problems with deployments to recovering sites after catastrophic failures, with much more in between. It would be great, though, if we could avoid some of these problems in the first place. In this chapter, we will discuss what can be done by Configuration Manager administrators to avoid getting into troublesome situations. It is important to get it right first time during the implementation. Afterward, you should monitor the site carefully and resolve issues before they become really troublesome.

We will examine the following topics in this chapter:

- Get it right at the start
- Tips to avoid trouble
- Monitoring the site
- Maintaining a healthy site

Get it right at the start

We've often attended customer sites where the Configuration Manager environment is performing poorly or has many issues. In many cases, the correct decisions were not made at the design stage. It's really difficult to recover from this, so it's vitally important to get it right from the start. We've included two of the main design errors that we see on a regular basis.

Hierarchy

It's very simple. There are very few reasons to deploy a **Central Administration Site (CAS)** unless you are managing a huge number of clients.

What is a CAS?

A CAS is the highest possible site server in a hierarchy. It is an optional component and is only required when you need to deploy multiple Primary Sites. The Primary Sites will be child sites of the CAS and will report their data to the CAS on a schedule.

Features of a CAS are as follows:

- Administration and reporting for the hierarchy
- You cannot assign clients to the CAS
- Does not process client data
- Does not support all site system roles
- Data is transferred from Primary Sites via SQL replication

Very few organizations will actually require a CAS in their hierarchy. With only a few exceptions, do *not* deploy a CAS and multiple Primary Sites unless you are managing over 150,000 clients (or expect to in the future).

In order to make decisions about your Configuration Manager Infrastructure design, you need to know the limitation for the number of supported clients in each scenario. The following table contains this information.

 Note that the numbers vary depending on the Configuration Manager version. Also, the table only contains full Windows clients. It does not include mobile devices.

Hierarchy design	Configuration Manager version	Supported number of clients
Stand-alone primary site	Prior to System Center 2012 Configuration Manager with SP2	100,000
	Beginning with System Center 2012 Configuration Manager SP2	150,000
CAS with Datacenter or Enterprise edition of SQL Server	Prior to System Center 2012 R2 Configuration Manager with cumulative update 3	400,000
	Beginning with System Center 2012 R2 Configuration Manager with cumulative update 3	500,000
	Beginning with System Center 2012 Configuration Manager SP2	600,000

Hierarchy design	Configuration Manager version	Supported number of clients
CAS with Standard edition of SQL Server	Configuration Manager (all versions)	50,000

Why do some administrators think that they need a CAS?

So why do some administrators think that they need to deploy a CAS in a smaller environment? We've encountered several explanations but very few are valid. Two valid reasons are, if you need to deploy the out of band service point and the Application Catalog web service point in an untrusted forest. They must be installed in the same forest as the site server.

We need a CAS because we have to manage clients in several different forests.

This is not the case. Configuration Manager is domain agnostic and a single Primary Site will easily manage clients across multiple forests (trusted or untrusted).

Having a CAS and two Primary sites gives me high availability options. I can fail clients over to the second Primary if one fails.

Not really, there is no automatic failover for clients between Primary sites.

We need a CAS so that teams can manage only the resources in their location.

This is not true either. You can implement **Role-Based Administration (RBA)** within a single Primary Site to achieve this.

We're not sure if we will need a CAS in the future so we better deploy it at the beginning.

Don't worry. With Configuration Manager 2012 SP1, you can now add a CAS afterward.

So why shouldn't you use a CAS?

When you implement a CAS in your hierarchy, you are introducing unnecessary complexity. Child Primary Sites pass their data to the CAS via SQL replication and this becomes the biggest troubleshooting issue in the environment. You will have to manage this environment on a daily basis. It requires constant attention and is better to be avoided if possible.

We've often encountered administrators (on Microsoft TechNet forums and customer sites) who made ill-informed decisions and now regret deploying a CAS.

You have been warned.

SQL server

Hopefully, by now, you have decided that you will be deploying a Primary Site only (unless you are one of the few administrators managing an environment of over 150,000 clients). The SQL server design and configuration will play a major part in how well this site will perform in the future. There are a number of decisions to be made.

Local or Remote SQL server?

This is a very common question at design stage. Our recommendation is that you install a SQL Server locally on the Site Server, as long as the server is suitably resourced, of course. Configuration Manager should then be installed on a dedicated SQL instance. The main reason for this is that you will have full control over the SQL database. Configuration Manager requires permissions over the database that Database Administrators can have a difficulty with. The Configuration Manager Site Server account must be a local administrator on the SQL server and sysadmin on the SQL instance. To avoid this regular ongoing dispute, it is much easier to install SQL on the Primary Site Server so that you are in control. We have come to this conclusion through the experience of many Configuration Manager implementations on customer sites.

One thing to be aware of if you decide on a local SQL installation is that, in some situations, you will reduce the number of clients that a site can manage. For example, a Child Primary Site with a local database can support up to 50,000 clients. This is usually enough for most organizations.

SQL Reporting can be a resource-intensive operation. On busy sites, it is often recommended to offload reporting operations by installing the **Reporting Service Point** on another server.

Drive configuration

It is best practice to install a SQL server using the configuration in the following table. It is also good practice to precreate the database files that will be used for Configuration Manager. Otherwise the installer will just automatically create a single database file.

Component	Recommendation
SQL Installation directory	Share with Configuration Manager directory. Do not use the `C:` drive for Program Files.
Database	Dedicated drive
Log files	Dedicated drive
TempDB	Dedicated drive
TempDB log files	Dedicated drive

Antivirus exclusions

It is vital to configure your antivirus solution to exclude specific files and folders from scanning in order for your Configuration Manager solution to perform optimally. You can find more information on antivirus exclusions as follows:

- SQL Server (`https://support.microsoft.com/en-us/kb/309422`)
- Configuration Manager (`http://blogs.technet.com/b/systemcenterpfe/archive/2013/01/11/updated-system-center-2012-configuration-manager-antivirus-exclusions-with-more-details.aspx`)

Tips to avoid trouble

In this section, we will look at some tips to avoid trouble with Configuration Manager. This information is from the field and we often encounter these problems when we visit customer sites.

Software Inventory

Software Inventory is a misnomer in Configuration Manager. The process should actually be called **File Inventory** because that's what it does. It collects information about files that are present on client systems. There are a few issues associated with the process and it is generally recommended not to use it in production sites.

- Even if a file exists on a system, it does not necessarily mean that a particular software is installed. It's much more accurate to use the information from **Add/Remove Programs**. This tells you exactly what software is installed on a system. Ironically, this information is collected by hardware inventory.

- By default, software inventory is not configured to do anything. You must add the file extensions for the files you wish to inventory. The more extensions you add, the more work you are asking a client to perform. When you factor in the influence of antivirus software, you could be causing performance issues on your clients for very little gain. In extreme circumstances, the inventory scan can time out and fail.

- All the pretty useless information you collect on every DLL and EXE in your environment must be written to the Configuration Manager database. This unnecessarily bloats the database. Please avoid doing that unless you have a good reason to do so.

 If you need to know if a specific DLL or EXE exists on your systems, it is recommended to use **Compliance** settings instead.

Deployments

As Configuration Manager administrators, we must take great care when creating deployments for our client estate. Any search engine will help you find some of the horror stories over the years where an administrator has wiped out an entire organization in a matter of minutes. They are not jokes. They are very real stories. Of course, it's easy to blame the technology when things go wrong. Basically though, Configuration Manager will only carry out the tasks that you tell it to do. It assumes that you know what you are doing and won't ask you if you are sure about a specific deployment.

Let's have a look at some deployment examples:

- Operating System Deployment task sequences
- Software Distribution
- Compliance settings

It's very important that you test your deployments carefully on a small number of test devices before you deploy to production devices.

Operating System Deployment task sequences

Operating System Deployment (**OSD**) can be the most dangerous. The first step in a task sequence is normally to format and partition the drive of the computer. If you deploy a Windows 8.1 installation task sequence to 500 servers, Configuration Manager will format and partition these servers without asking for permission. You must be very careful when you deploy these task sequences.

Microsoft has recently introduced a feature to prompt you to think carefully when you are deploying an OSD task sequence. A dialog box tells you that this is a potentially high risk deployment.

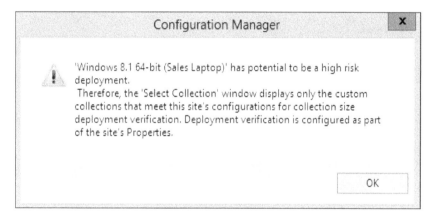

By default, you are only presented with a choice of collections that contain 100 clients or less. You have to uncheck a box in order to choose a collection with more than 100 computers. Please be careful.

It's common practice to deploy operating systems using PXE. Administrators only have to press *F12* on the keyboard to invoke network booting and reimage a computer. It is important to password protect PXE to prevent unauthorized users from reimaging computers.

Software distribution

Configuration Manager allows us to create requirement rules when we are deploying applications. They are very useful if you want to limit the deployment to devices based on some criteria. For example, you may want to deploy a marketing application to all marketing users. However, you know that this application is quite resource intensive, so you don't want to install on computers that have less than 4 GB RAM.

Follow these steps to create a requirement rule:

1. Select the **Requirements** tab in the **Deployment Type** for the application.

2. Click on **Add** to create a requirement rule.

3. Enter your requirement as shown in the following screenshot:

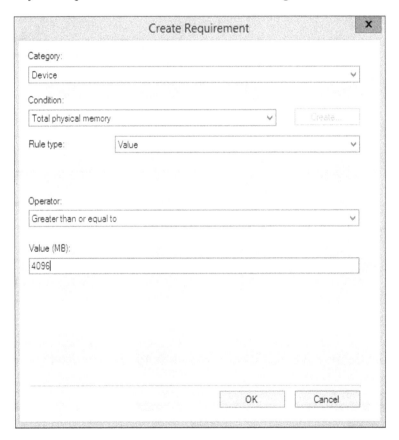

Compliance settings

Configuration Manager is a powerful tool. It allows you to deploy a common compliance baseline to your estate of servers and desktops. You can control many features and settings of the devices including registry settings.

Please do not deploy compliance settings to your devices without thorough testing. Your test collection should not just include computers in the IT department (this is often the case as you don't mind breaking them). This is not a true test. You must choose computers from all aspects of the business as these computers can include specialist applications — human resources, finance, marketing, and so on. In this way, you have a better chance of identifying an issue before mass deployment.

Software updates

Troubleshooting the software updates process was previously discussed in *Chapter 7, Troubleshooting Common Tasks*. It is a complicated process with many components working together to secure your environment against vulnerabilities.

Great care must be taken when you deploy a software update solution. We've included some items here that you should be aware of when configuring your solution.

Disable Automatic Updates

When you configure your Configuration Manager solution for software updates, a local policy is created on each client. The policy shows that Configuration Manager is now the authority for software updates. However, in the event that this policy was somehow not applied, the **Windows Updates** settings could revert to their default. The default is for each client to contact the Microsoft Updates site and download and install updates at 3 am. This is an unlikely occurrence but it has happened. On a large site, this can cause major Internet access issues.

It is good practice to create a **Group Policy Object** (**GPO**) to remove this risk. The GPO should be configured to do one of the following:

- Configure the WSUS server
- Disable Automatic Updates on your clients

The first option is the preferred option as, in this case, the Windows Update Agent can still be updated if necessary.

Maintenance Windows

It's common practice to deploy software updates to desktops with a forced deadline sometime in the future. This works well for desktops. Users get regular notifications that updates are available and are prompted to install them and reboot their computers. When the deadline is reached, the updates are forcibly installed by Configuration Manager and the computer is rebooted.

However, you cannot adopt this approach with servers. Use **Maintenance Windows (MWs)** to prevent servers being rebooted during business hours. Ensure that you configure the MWs to be long enough for all updates to be installed.

Be careful when you are configuring the window. As we know, software updates are generally released on the second Tuesday of every month. If you want to start installing updates on your servers the next evening, it would make sense to configure a monthly MW starting on the second Wednesday of every month (see the following screenshot). However, that will not work for you. The second Wednesday of the month is not always after the second Tuesday. This is a very common mistake.

It is recommended to use a PowerShell script instead to create the monthly MWs as you need them. You can find the PowerShell cmdlet reference for Configuration Manager 2012 R2 in this TechNet library document at `https://technet.microsoft.com/en-us/library/jj821831%28v=sc.20%29.aspx?f=255&MSPPErr or=-2147217396`.

Collections

On occasions we encounter sites that are experiencing delays in updating collection memberships. This can be a result of poor database performance, so you should reindex the database in the first instance (this should be a regular routine in any case).

The Configuration Manager 2012 R2 Toolkit includes a new tool called the **Collection Evaluation Viewer**. You can use the tool to examine the various queues that are used for Collection Evaluation. You can find useful information such as **Run Time**, **Last Evaluation Completion Time**, **Next Evaluation Time**, and **Member Changes**. These can be used to troubleshoot poor collection evaluation performance.

You can also examine the `colleval.log` file that records details about when collections are created, changed, and deleted by the Collection Evaluator.

It is also possible that you have configured incremental updates on a large number of collections. It is recommended to only configure incremental updates on approximately 200 collections in your hierarchy. It is very difficult to define the exact number as this depends on several factors such as the following:

- The total number of collections in your hierarchy
- How frequently you are adding and removing resources
- Number of clients
- Complexity of collection membership rules

Wake-up proxy

Wake-up proxy, introduced with Configuration Manager 2012 SP1, checks if computers on a subnet are awake, and wakes them if required. This technology has been a little controversial and carries a very strong warning in the Microsoft documentation.

During the process, wake-up proxy informs the network switch that a spoofed network adapter is connected to a particular port, and this is not the network adapter expected and registered to that port. This behavior is called **MAC flapping** and is not normal in network operations.

Switches from many vendors will not support MAC flapping. The switch will not understand how it is receiving packets from two different interfaces with the same source MAC address. It specifically causes a problem when port security has been enabled on the switch. This feature can lead to major networking outages if not planned and implemented correctly.

Monitoring the site

A Configuration Manager infrastructure is quite robust. However, occasionally things do go wrong. It is not a good position to be in when something fails unexpectedly. At this stage, there is panic and confusion and it's difficult to troubleshoot under these circumstances.

It's much better to be proactive rather than reactive. Configuration Manager monitoring is an important part of an administrator's job.

Monitor Configuration Manager Sites

Use the **Monitoring** workspace in the Configuration Manager console to monitor the hierarchy and associated operations. Additionally, there are many reports and log files designed to assist you in maintaining a healthy environment. The following should be carefully considered when monitoring a Configuration Manager hierarchy:

- Status messages with errors and warnings
- Event log errors on site systems
- SQL errors
- Poor SQL performance
- Excessive file backlog on site systems
- Network issues
- Inactive clients

Monitor WAN links

When you are designing a Configuration Manager infrastructure, it's vital to consider how you will manage remote sites without causing excessive bandwidth usage. The solution must be designed based on the number of users in each site and the quality of the WAN link to that site. You also must factor in what management features you will be using. Will you be deploying operating system images at the remote site, for example?

If you have a remote location with a large number of users, you may decide to deploy a Secondary Site. This supports up to a maximum of 5,000 users (or up to 10,000 from Configuration Manager 2012 SP2).

But what do you do if you don't have that many users? Our recommendation is to deploy a remote DP in sites that have 20 or more users. You can configure rate limits and schedules to protect the bandwidth during business hours.

However, some organizations make the decision of not to deploy any site systems in some remote sites initially. In these cases, it's very important to monitor the WAN link for excessive network activity, especially if you are carrying out OSDs. This can adversely affect network connectivity between sites.

Monitor Distribution Points

If you deploy remote DPs, you must ensure that they are performing reliably so that Configuration Manager clients have access to content when required. There are a number of tools we can use to monitor DPs.

Configuration Manager Console

Monitor the DP status using the Configuration Manager console as follows:

- Navigate to **Monitoring** | **Overview** | **System Status** | **Site Status**. Verify that all your DPs have enough free disk space.

- Navigate to **Monitoring** | **Overview** | **System Status** | **Component** Status. Check the messages associated with the SMS_Distribution_Manager component.

- Navigate to **Monitoring** | **Overview** | **Distribution Status** | **Distribution Point Configuration Status**. Check for warnings.

- Navigate to **Monitoring** | **Overview** | **Reporting** | **Reports**. Run the Software Distribution — content report.

Log files

Review the following log files on the Site Server:

- DistMgr.log: This log records details about package creation, replication, and information updates.

- PkgXferMgr.log: This log records the actions of the SMS Executive component, which is responsible for content distribution from primary to remote sites.

Distribution Point Job Manager

The DP Job Manager is included as part of the Configuration Manager 2012 R2 toolkit. It will assist you in managing and troubleshooting ongoing content distribution jobs. It even allows you to control the priority of current jobs.

System Center Operations Manager

You would imagine that the best way to monitor a Microsoft technology is with another Microsoft technology, and you would be right. We recommend that you monitor the health of your entire environment (not just the Configuration Manager infrastructure) with **System Center Operations Manager (SCOM)**.

SCOM is a robust monitoring solution. It can be deployed as it is highly available and provides comprehensive monitoring for your critical systems. It uses Management Packs (MPs), which are designed to focus on a particular service or technology. Microsoft has developed a Management Pack that allows you to monitor the health of the Configuration Manager environment.

You can download the System Center Monitoring Pack for System Center 2012 – Configuration Manager from `http://www.microsoft.com/en-us/download/details.aspx?id=29267`.

The link also allows you to download two very detailed and informative documents which is as follows:

- Monitoring Pack Contents for System Center 2012 Configuration Manager: This guide provides a very detailed list of the monitors, rules, and reports that are available for the various Configuration Manager components.

- Guide for System Center Monitoring Pack for System Center 2012 Configuration Manager: This guide provides general information on monitoring scenarios and configuration options.

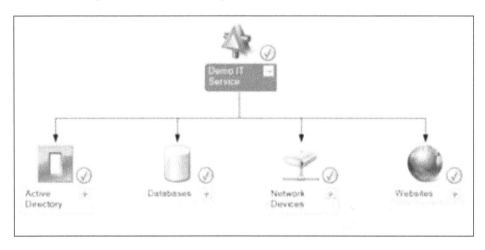

Maintaining a healthy site

This section describes some general tasks that a Configuration Manager administrator should carry out in order to maintain a healthy site. Housekeeping is a very important aspect of the job.

Database indexing

Fragmented indexes cause performance issues with SQL databases, and it gets worse over time. It is crucial to perform regular reindexing of the Configuration Manager database. How will you know if you have excessive fragmentation? Execute the following T-SQL command on your database:

`DBCC Showcontig`

You can see the results of this command in a test lab shown in the following screenshot. In the lab, there is no issue with fragmentation. However, it's very different in the real world. If the site database is fragmented more than 10 percent, then you need to take action and rebuild the indexes:

You could configure the built-in database reindexing maintenance task. However, in our opinion, this is not the optimal solution. It is more efficient to use a script developed by Ola Hallengren MVP. This is widely regarded as the optimal solution for SQL Server Index and Statistics Maintenance which can be found at `http://ola.hallengren.com/sql-server-index-and-statistics-maintenance.html`.

Steve Thompson MVP offers some advice on using this script for indexing the Configuration Manager database. You will find that at `https://stevethompsonmvp.wordpress.com/2013/05/07/optimizing-configmgr-databases/`.

WSUS Server Cleanup Utility

The SUSDB database is the fundamental component of the Configuration Manager/ WSUS software updates solution. If you are updating multiple products, then this database can grow very large in size. You should run regular cleanup jobs on that database.

WSUS Server Cleanup is used to help you manage your disk space. It carries out the following functions:

- Remove unused updates and update revisions
- Delete obsolete computers
- Delete unnecessary update files
- Decline expired updates
- Decline superseded updates

It's highly recommended to run the wizard using PowerShell. Use the `Invoke-WsusServerCleanup` command in conjunction with some of the additional parameters shown in the following screenshot:

```
PS C:\Users\admingerry> get-help Invoke-WsusServerCleanup

NAME
    Invoke-WsusServerCleanup

SYNTAX
    Invoke-WsusServerCleanup [-UpdateServer <IUpdateServer>] [-CleanupObsoleteComputers] [-CleanupObsoleteUpdates]
    [-CleanupUnneededContentFiles] [-CompressUpdates] [-DeclineExpiredUpdates] [-DeclineSupersededUpdates] [-WhatIf]
    [-Confirm] [<CommonParameters>]
```

Inactive clients

This is one of the more difficult tasks facing a Configuration Manager administrator. It's very important that the client information is as accurate and up to date as possible. Otherwise it can be very difficult for you. You'll have problems maintaining software updates compliance, for example, if many of the computers don't actually exist. Also, what can we do when clients appear as inactive?

A client is active if it can be discovered and remains in communication with the Configuration Manager environment. By default, the heartbeat discovery runs once every 7 days.

The following tasks should be carried out:

- Active Directory cleanup (you can use DSQuery commands to find and disable stale computer accounts)
- Delete Aged Discovery Data Site Maintenance task
- Delete Inactive Client Discovery Data Site Maintenance task

One of the more useful community tools for working with clients is the Client Center for Configuration Manager which can be found at `http://sccmclictr.codeplex.com`.

Summary

In this chapter, we discussed how to avoid trouble in our Configuration Manager environment. We stressed the importance of getting it right first time and highlighted some important design decisions that can haunt you at a later stage. We offered some tips on avoiding trouble in everyday administration.

Then we talked about the importance of monitoring the various components in your environment and being proactive rather than reactive. Finally, we discussed some regular housekeeping tasks that should be carried out in order to maintain a healthy site.

We hope that this information is helpful to you to keep out of trouble.

Index

www.ingramcontent.com/pod-product-compliance
Lightning Source LLC
Chambersburg PA
CBHW082117070326
40690CB00049B/3584